FOOD
Past, Present and Future

FOOD
Past, Present and Future

Egon Larsen

Illustrations by

DAVID ARMITAGE

FREDERICK MULLER LIMITED
LONDON

First published in Great Britain 1977
by Frederick Muller Limited,
London NW2 6LE

ISBN: 0 584 10293 3

British Library Cataloguing in Publication Data

Larsen, Egon
    Food.
    1. Food — History
    I. Title
    641.3'009   TX353

    ISBN 0—584—10293—3

Printed in Great Britain by Clarke, Doble & Brendon Ltd., Plymouth
and bound by G & J Kitcat Ltd London S.E.1

CONTENTS

"First let's have grub, and morals afterwards."

Bertolt Brecht
(*Threepenny Opera*)

1

HOW FOOD CHANGED MAN

Half a Million Years Ago

The tallest animal on earth, the giraffe, likes to feed on the young leaves of the highest tree branches. It can do this easily because of its long neck. There is a fundamental question which comes to mind: does the giraffe prefer that particular fare because those top leaves are well within reach of its mouth, thanks to the long neck? Or has the giraffe, in the course of evolution, developed its long neck so that it can get at the kind of food it wants?

We may never know for sure. All we know is that in the struggle for survival the fittest win. Being fit to survive means for a species that a sufficient number of its members reach the age of mating and procreation. This may involve adaptation to new conditions. The big saurians, or giant lizards, which developed and lived long before man appeared on our planet, eventually died out: they were unfit to survive, probably because they were unable to adapt to changing climatic conditions which also changed the available kinds of food.

Survival or extinction, therefore, depends largely on nourishment. Creatures which developed their alimentary organs for a certain kind of fare often had to alter their feeding habits in order to survive when circumstances changed, and man has been no exception. He has, however, one organ which helps him to reorganize his way of life if this becomes necessary: a thinking brain, with two 'executive organs' for carrying out his thoughts: his hands.

But it would be wrong to assume that man made full use of these advantages over the rest of the animal kingdom as soon as he appeared, about half a million years ago, on the scene as *homo erectus*. His primitive mind did not, at first, give much thought to the whole subject of food — he just ate what he found:

7

plants and roots, birds' eggs and fruits; and he killed for food what he could with his bare hands: small game and shellfish, snakes and insects. He learnt by experience which plants and animals were harmful, and which were suitable for eating.

Then, gradually, his brain began to think of ways to improve his gathering of desirable foodstuffs. Like the higher-organized apes — whom we can watch doing this in the zoo — he began to extend the range of his arms by using sticks, for instance, to knock down fruit from trees. The next step must have been the use of sticks and stones for killing animals for food or in defence. Perhaps the change from moving on all fours to walking upright

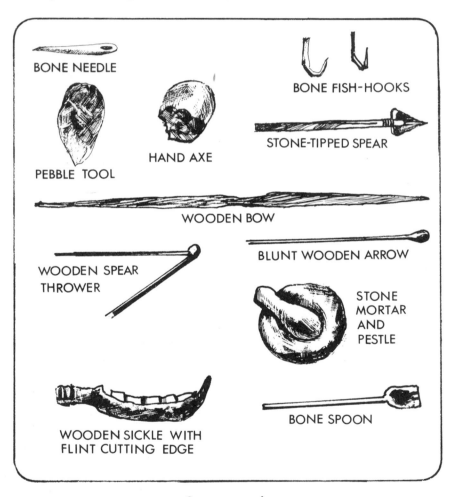

Stone age tools

had come with learning to throw rocks at animals — he had to have his hands free for the purpose, and he could see further standing on his feet.

As man's brain and fingers developed he was able to chip flint stones into shape and sharpen them to form weapons such as spearheads, axes, and knives. Stone age man — who lived tens of thousands of years ago — became a hunter and later, when he had invented hooks and harpoons, a fisher. Eventually he discovered that he could extend his range of action even further by means of bows and arrows.

After the weapons came the first tools, also made of flint stones: spades for digging up roots, planes for shaping wood, needles for fastening the animal skins he used as garments, and even primitive surgical instruments. We cannot tell when and where these inventions were made — probably at different times and among various human tribes. Nor do we know the place and time of the first use of fire for warming and lighting up man's cave homes and for cooking food; this vital development in prehistory must also have occurred in a number of different places and many times, again and again. At any rate, after thousands of years of eating raw food man discovered that cooked meals were a great deal more digestible and agreeable, and that roasting — and later boiling — his food greatly extended the range of animal flesh and plants he could digest.

This was important for man's survival as a species, for his food choice had been rather limited so long as he ate it raw. Wild animals' flesh is rather muscular and tough, and man's teeth — though in those early periods stronger and sharper than they are now — could not cope with it very well; nor did he possess a powerful gizzard like some kinds of birds, in which hard grains are prepared for digestion, or a 'chain' of stomachs like the ruminants, which enables them to live on raw plants. Cooking made a great number of potential foodstuffs usable for humans, thus saving them from probable extinction during the ice ages.

When man discovered the technique of using fire for cooking, he added not only to the quantity of available food: today we know that cooking works all kinds of beneficial changes in foodstuffs. Harmful bacteria in meat and poisonous elements in some plants are destroyed by the heat. By boiling meat, juices are extracted from it, and the starch in grains becomes digestible by the same process.* And we must not underrate the extra

* For more details, see Chapter IV.

benefit man derived by cooking food: the discovery that eating can be more than just a means of keeping body and soul together — that it can also be a pleasure. This, perhaps, was the beginning of civilization; it was certainly the beginning of the art of cookery.

The Great Revolution

The human race was now firmly established on our planet. Originally, most tribes may have got their fire from trees which had been struck by lightning; they learnt how to keep it burning and how to transfer it to their caves. Then they began to experiment and found ways of starting fires of their own by rubbing pieces of dry wood together or by striking sparks from flint, setting dry grass alight.

Throughout that early phase, the hunting and fishing tribes used to migrate, following the animals that served as their main food from region to region according to the seasons. More permanent settlements were established at the seaside where fish could be caught throughout the year, and here the first means of transport was invented — the boat, starting with dug-out canoes made from tree trunks. They were most useful for off-shore fishing with spears and hooks, thus adding to the tribes' seafood diet which had at first consisted mainly of edible fish that could be collected on the beaches: crabs and mussels, clams and shrimps. An important innovation, probably first used by tribes which had settled around the Baltic 9000 years ago, was the fishing net made of bass (or bast), the inner bark of the lime tree.

The last of the ice ages which humans had survived in the Northern Hemisphere ended about 15,000 years ago, but they kept on living in caves and gathering their food as hunters and fishers. It was in the more clement climate of the Middle East that Stone age man found some 10,000 years ago, another possible way of life, and a better one than the arduous and precarious existence of a wandering hunter: he became a farmer.

This was, without doubt, the greatest revolution in the history of mankind. It marked the end of constant migration and the beginning of continuous habitations in the food-producing areas. Houses were built, villages grew and became towns, with communities which eventually united, under efficient leaders, into nations and states. During the first seven thousand years of farming, the population of the ancient world increased from about three million to some hundred million people.

How did farming begin? One theory is that the women of the

hunting groups, who as a rule gathered the edible plants for the family, discovered the connection between new growth and seeds, which they began to sow at places where the wandering tribe expected to stay for a few months. Then the men joined them in their efforts; they learnt to till the ground, to plant and to reap, and — most important — to irrigate the soil. New kinds of tools had to be made: the plough, the hoe, the sickle, the spade; metals — bronze, copper, tin, and later iron — began to be used for utensils, for pots and pans, and for weapons. The power of the fire was harnessed for shaping them by smelting and forging.

At first the farmer himself dragged the plough through the soil, as he still does in primitive countries. But in many areas, he trained oxen to help him. He tamed the ass and much later the horse to pull his cart and to let him ride on their backs. Life became easier, food more varied and plentiful; instead of hunting meat-producing animals, the farmer domesticated certain species and reared herds of them for food: cattle, sheep, goats, pigs. They were given shelters. Building grew into a specialized craft.

The houses which the tribes built when they settled permanently were at first no more than mud huts; then, when suitable tools had been developed, stone was used for building. Wooden houses were probably first built by tribes who settled on the Alpine lakes and on islands in the South Seas; they were erected on piles rammed into the marshy ground. Eventually, man learnt to make bricks of sun-dried clay and straw, and began to use them as basic building units.

The technique of pottery, which provided the early kitchens with earthenware vessels for carrying and storing food, had already begun in the late Stone age and developed into a fine art around the eastern shores of the Mediterranean after the invention of the potter's wheel. Grinding the corn, especially for making flour, also started in the late Stone age as man's diet was including more and more cooked meals; in the beginning, it was just a laborious pounding of the grain, usually done by the women, until the ingenious invention of the wheel prompted that of the revolving millstone which could also be operated by tamed animals.

The farmer, the miller, the potter, the baker, the tinsmith and other occupations connected with food and cooking gradually developed as separate trades, and eventually merchants took over the business of buying up, transporting, storing and selling food supplies. Drink, however, was for a long period provided by the families of the farmers: the women fetched the water and the men brewed the beer; five or four thousand years ago it was already the most popular drink in Babylon and in Egypt. As the towns grew and the range of thirst-making, spiced dishes extended, brewing also became a specialized occupation; the Egyptian Pharaohs established state-run breweries. The vintner's trade, on the other hand, has always been a distinctive craft right from the discovery — we don't know how many millennia ago — that the fermented juice of grapes makes not only a thirst-quenching, delicious drink but also a means of raising man's spirits. However, so long as the tribes were migrating they had no wine; growing it ties the vintner to the soil, to certain features of the landscape. Vines need tending and grapes must be processed; permanent settlements were therefore an essential condition for the cultivation of vineyards.

The traders, or merchants, whom we have mentioned, appeared on the scene relatively late. During the early stages of village life, these little communities were self-supporting, consuming only what they themselves produced. Then they began to barter with neighbouring villages, exchanging surplus produce. It seems that the invention of money was made no earlier than about 700 B.C., probably by the Lydians who lived in what is now south-western Turkey; thier last king, by the way, was the proverbially rich Croesus. They struck coins which were accepted in place of goods throughout Lydia and soon also in neighbouring regions; but there the rulers saw no reason why they should not coin their own money from metals found in their own areas. By 500 B.C., all the Greek city states had their own mints and currencies.

The general acceptance of coinage had a marked effect on the food scene. The merchants multiplied, and so did the exchange of produce. Foodstuffs, delicacies and particularly spices from other countries could now be bought on the markets in the towns and inspired the cooks' imagination. Even more important, spices helped to preserve foodstuffs and to disguise the unpleasant taste and smell of meat and vegetables which were no longer fresh.

Bad taste and smell, of course, are warning signals that the food is deteriorating, and man learnt by bitter experience about its dangers to health. The tribes that had settled and were no longer living from hand to mouth were faced with the problem of food preservation. Harvested crops had to be made to last for months to avoid famine. Early rulers made their people build granaries; fish was dried or smoked to stave off the process of rotting, and meat was found to remain edible for a longer period when it was

A sacrificial altar

salted. In fact, salt became a most valuable commodity in inland regions which had no access to the salt-producing sea but had to rely on supplies from salt mines. The salt trade was one of the first important inter-regional economic activities; many European settlements grew into towns thanks to their situations on salt trade routes. Bridges were built and tolls demanded from the salt traders who wanted to cross them.

Food, Faith, and Magic

To primitive man, every natural phenomenon was inextricably part of a supernatural system. Gods and spirits were everywhere; they controlled all human life, the weather, plant growth, personal luck and misfortune, the tribe's victory or defeat in war. Certain animals were considered sacred; certain kinds of food endowed man with magical powers or at least with sexual potency — a vital necessity for the survival of the tribe. Eating and drinking was important not just for filling the stomach; by absorbing food and drink in his own body, man was incorporating some part of nature, transferring its characteristics into himself. The extreme expression of this belief is cannibalism, still being practised in remote regions of Indonesia, New Guinea, and South America: not because a tribe is starving but because of the magical powers the man-eater hopes to acquire over his dead enemies' spirits.

There is still a strong element of belief in the magical 'transubstantiation' of bread and wine in the Roman-Catholic Eucharist: by virtue of consecration, bread and wine change into the body and blood of Christ, symbolizing Holy Communion. The 'host', the consecrated bread, derives its name from *hostia*, the Latin word for a lamb when offered in sacrifice. The pre-Christian gods were presumed to like offerings of food and drink. Animals, birds, corn, and fruit were sacrificed; the Romans poured out wine ('libation') at their meals in honour of the household gods, the Israelites and other tribes poured oil or wine on their altars — a practice which has still not died out among modern Africans.

But these offerings were already a substitute for the much older rite of immolating live human beings. The dramatic end of that barbaric custom, at least among the Jews, had been recorded in the Old Testament: first the Lord demands of Abraham the sacrifice of his only son, Isaac, as a test of his faith; then, when Abraham has already raised his knife to kill the boy, an angel appears and tells him to stop and sacrifice instead a ram as his burnt offering. The basic idea of a sacrifice was to 'buy' atonement for sin, placate the deity, prove one's loyalty to it, and ensure future good luck by offering something of value, such as food. Aaron, the brother of Moses and High Priest of the Israelites at their exodus from Egypt, was commanded by God to make a daily burnt offering of two lambs, plus fine flour mixed with pure olive oil, and wine as a libation. It was a real sacrifice for the fugitives who were often short of food on their wanderings.

Food played an important spiritual role in biblical times, and it still does in the life of an orthodox Jew. In remembrance of that exodus, for instance, he still eats only unleavened bread (*matzoh*) during the Passover feast because the Children of Israel had to get out of Egypt in such a hurry that they had no time to leaven their dough for the journey — incidentally, the leavening of the bread dough was probably an Egyptian invention. Then, on their travels across the desert, when the Jews were starving and almost rebelled against their exacting leader Moses, the Lord sent them Manna from heaven. It was perhaps the gummy, sweetish exudation from the tamarisk shrubs of Mount Sinai, or some edible lichen loosened from the rocks by the wind and carried by it to the hungry tribe.

Moses, who was not only a brilliant military and administrative leader but also a shrewd psychologist, laid down an elaborate system of food laws for his people. Much of it may have originated in ancient superstitions, taboos, and magical beliefs, but there are also a good many rules that make sense, such as the ban on eating pork. It was the favourite kind of meat among many Middle and Far-Eastern peoples because pigs are easy to raise. But already the Egyptians had banned it, and Moses took his cue from them because in a hot climate pigs may become infected with trichinosis, which causes severe sickness in humans who eat pork and can result in death. Similar medical reasons, though mixed with pagan superstitions, seem to have made Moses and his

14

advisers draw up that long list of 'clean' and 'unclean' food animals we find in the Bible. Yet the ban on consuming blood, another basic rule of *kosher* (Hebrew for 'right') slaughter, cooking, and eating, is probably founded on ancient magical notions — while fasting on a holy day is a sensible health rule still valid in our age of slimming cures.

Dogs were eaten in the Stone Age; in China, chows used to be bred as a culinary speciality. The Polynesians and some African tribes still eat dogflesh. The horse, which came to the Middle East and Europe from Mongolia, was eaten wherever horses were bred; in France and Belgium there are still butcher's shops which sell only horsemeat. The Teutonic priests in ancient Germany fancied it more than any other meat and forbade the common people to eat it: a taboo which continued even after that country had become Christian. Hinduism, which originated in the sixth century B.C., banned any slaughter of cattle, and cows are still 'holy' to its adherents.

Magical notions, especially the belief in witchcraft among primitive peoples, have always been widespread with regard to food. There is, for instance, the ancient belief that a man's soul may 'escape' through his mouth when he is eating or drinking; among some tribes it is customary to cover one's face when the mouth is opened to prevent the soul from coming out and getting into some enemy's power. Misfortunes and bad health are often blamed on spells put on food by witches or malevolent opponents. No doubt, African voodoo and juju 'magic' can make people sick or even kill them if they believe strongly enough in such evil spells.

On the other hand, there is an age-old belief in the magical qualities of certain plants such as the mandrake (or mandragora). The roots of this Mediterranean plant, which has narcotic properties, faintly resemble the human body, and were said to shriek when pulled out of the ground. Eating them was believed to increase a man's sexual powers and a woman's fecundity; drinking the juice was said to produce sweet dreams — effects which are mentioned in Genesis and in some Shakespeare plays. Beetroot juice, because it is red, was thought to cure anaemia, and celandine flowers, because they are yellow, were said to be a cure for jaundice. Fish, it is still widely believed, improves our brain; in fact, it contains phosphorus which the brain needs. There is also a kernel of truth in the ancient Egyptian notion that eating ox liver cures night-blindness: liver (like carrots) contains Vitamin A, which helps us to see better at night.

What the Ancients Ate

We know from the Bible much about the everyday diet of the people around the eastern shores of the Mediterranean in antiquity. Barley bread was their staple food; meat, milk, and cheese was provided by the herds of cattle, sheep, asses, and goats, and they kept chickens. Lentils and beans were the main kinds of vegetables, figs the favourite fruit, honey the chief ingredient of the sweet-meats. Olive oil was used for cooking. In most regions, wine was not regarded as a luxury, but as a feature of the daily meal. Special delicacies among some tribes in the Middle East were snails and fried grasshoppers. Among the spices used extensively in cooking, caraway, coriander, and garlic were early favourites.

Besides grape wine — and in some countries beer — palm and date wine were popular alcoholic drinks. Wine was also made from elderberries, strawberries, and other kinds of fruit. The Germanic tribes were said to be particularly fond of mead, fermented wild honey mixed with water; the Tartars and Kalmuks favoured *koumiss,* the fermented milk of mares, and the American Indians invented *paiwari,* made from manioc — their women chewed the roots and spat them into a trough, where they fermented.

The royal tombs of the Egyptians reveal a great deal about their food habits as well as about the marked class distinctions in that society. The common people and the slaves lived on a frugal diet of dark bread and gruel, fish, beans, onions, and dates; meat was a rare luxury. In contrast, the upper classes fed sumptuously. Tomb pictures dating from the fourth dynasty, six thousand years ago, show nine kinds of meat, many kinds of bread and cake, various poultry dishes, grapes, plums, figs, melons, apricots, butter, onions, milk and wine — all being served at one meal. Food was buried with the dead as provisions for their journey to the beyond and as offerings to the gods.

The ancient Greeks were no great innovators in the field of cooking and eating; indeed, the Spartans, the people of the Peloponnese peninsula, regarded asceticism as a virtue and over-eating as a vice because it would impair a man's military prowess. There were periods in Spartan history when the citizens were forced to have their meals at public tables, with 'black broth' as the main dish — a concoction so repulsive that foreigners who had tasted it said that they now understood why Spartans preferred dying in battle to living on black broth.

To the well-to-do Atheneans, food was much less important than art and philosophy; their social gatherings were not gastronomical feasts but *symposia,* drinking-parties with intellectual conversations, or music and dancers. Their meals were somewhat monotonous; the meat was mainly pork, but the emphasis was on fish; of which a variety were eaten. The reason was probably that the Greek soil is meagre and does not produce much for a luxurious table while the coastline is long and rich in natural harbours.

The Greeks, who liked to apply philosophy to everyday life, devised a peculiar system of classifying foodstuffs. They were thinking in terms of the 'four elements' — air, water, fire, and earth — whose qualities were attributed to foodstuffs: cool = air, moist = water, hot = fire, dry = earth. Foods, the Greeks reasoned, were combinations of these elements, and different circumstances and kinds of people required different combinations. Healthy people, for instance, needed other food combinations than sick ones, and the nature of an illness indicated the patient's requirements, such as 'cool' food for people with 'hot' blood.

Despite their more realistic way of thinking, the Romans took over this strange Greek food philosophy, and it persisted throughout Europe right up to the end of the seventeenth century. Doctors classified their patients according to their 'cardinal humours': blood, phlegm, choler or yellow bile, melancholy or black bile. The patient's diet was prescribed accordingly. The whole of the original Greek system fitted well into the medieval Christian view that everything in the world was meant for the good of man, and that God had created plants to cure every disease. It was the herbalist's task to identify them, not only by their effects on the patient but also by their appearance — a system called the 'Doctrine of Signatures'. For instance, hepatica, the liverwort, had liver-shaped leaves to represent the organ for which it was beneficial; the 'flesh' of the walnut looked like a brain, so that was the organ it could cure; and as the saxifrage grew among the rocks it was a remedy for gall or kidney stones. There were also other bits of medieval medical advice connected with food, which sound rather puzzling today — such as healing burns with lettuce soaked in a woman's milk.

In the seventeenth century, Nicholas Culpeper, the popular medical writer, complicated matters even more by linking herbs with astrology.

But let us return to the ancient Greeks. The lower classes in their society — mainly peasants and slaves — had little opportunity of choosing their food according to the philosophers' theories. They had to be content with getting enough *maza* for their hungry stomachs. This staple food was a barley cake, certainly no delicacy

17

even when mixed with honey; which has always been a cheap commodity in Greece. Other poor men's dishes were barley porridge with goat's milk and wheat gruel with eggs beaten into it. Cheese, too, was popular and cheap, made from the milk of goats and sheep. Olive oil was used in cooking, never butter. Grapes and figs were eaten fresh and dried. Meat was too expensive for the lower orders.

There was one Greek community whose name became synonymous for excesses of the table: the Sybarites. But they did not live in Greece proper; Sybaris was a Greek colony in southern Italy, grown wealthy by efficient trading in foreign spices and delicacies. The Sybarite cooks used them for creating fabulous meals. No wonder the neighbouring colonies envied and hated the Sybarites, and in the end their city was attacked and razed to the ground.

So long as Rome was a small republic fighting hard for survival and extending its rule only gradually over the whole of Italy, the Romans lived frugally; their meals were rather less substantial than those of the Italian peasants, and there was no great difference between a patrician and a plebeian dinner. The staple food was brown or black bread; gruel, home-grown vegetables and fruit, modest helpings of pork and poultry, and small kinds of fish were the usual components of a middle-class meal. The slaves, antiquity's working-class, had to live on a more austere diet.

There were frequent food shortages, especially as a result of wars, in the city of Rome, with price rises that roused the anger of the population. This was dangerous for the governing Senate, and food aid for the lower classes became a necessary feature of the Roman establishment. Gaius Gracchus, the controversial 'tribune of the plebs' in the second century B.C., permitted the people to buy grain at cheap nominal prices from the state granaries to prevent food riots. Fifty years later, during another economic crisis, free grain distribution was introduced for the first time; it remained a permanent form of social assistance for centuries. There were times when no less than a third of the population received free grain and other foodstuffs, even after Rome had already grown into an empire ruling not only the Mediterranean area but also the rest of the ancient world, from the Caspian Sea to the borders of Caledonia. That was the time when Roman upper-class appetites had increased immensely with all these conquests and their riches: the time of the famous Roman cuisine.

One must not forget, however, that excesses of the table were confined to a minority of Romans, the imperial families, the very rich, the powerful public figures. The sophistication of Roman cooking did not lead to any lasting improvement in nutrition, nor to any general rise in the standard of ordinary people's diet. What we now admire as a great era of the culinary art in antiquity began only in the last century before the birth of Christ and lasted for less than 300 years; then the first deep cracks showed in the imperial edifice, and the Roman conquerors were too worried about their external and internal security to devote a great deal of thought and money to their cuisine. When Rome's empire was gone, so were its feasts.

Still, it was a fascinating show. A wealthy Roman — such as the General and gourmet Lucullus — would work up an appetite for the big evening meal during the day by having just a drink for breakfast and a snack at midday. At night, the family and their guests would assemble in the dining hall with its large couches, where they would all recline on mattresses and cushions, eating with their fingers and with knives and spoons. In the middle between the couches was an enormous table to which the food was brought by the slaves. They handed it around on plates and poured the wine, and they also brought the diners perfumed water for washing their fingers.

The meal began with a libation to the *lares,* the household deities. For 'starters' there were light dishes such as eggs, oysters, and salads. The first main course was usually pork or some other roast meat; hosts who wanted to show off had a whole boar served

Roman feast

up — or even two or three boars for a large party. Other meat dishes were more outlandish, for instance dormice fattened for the table with acorns or chestnuts, and occasionally camel meat — not forgetting the heels, which were much appreciated by gourmets.

Next came a poultry dish, though rarely chicken, which was considered too commonplace for the rich. Peacocks were served with all their feathers stuck on again after cooking. Quails and smaller birds were regarded as delicacies and killed by their hundreds for banquets; large birds such as cranes, storks, and even flamingoes and ostriches were favourite treats, especially their brains and tongues.

Fish dishes were at first not as popular with the Romans as they were with the Greeks, but in imperial times Roman cooks learned to prepare sturgeon, pike, mullet, and turbot for the gourmets. Fish was often served with fruit purees and sweet-sour sauces made from honey, vinegar, and currants. Sauces were stored in stone jars in the cellars. Salted and dried fish was considered rather plebeian by the wealthy Romans, but the lower classes ate much of it because it was cheap.

As to vegetables and salads, the Romans liked leeks and lettuce, cauliflowers and olives, celery and beans, chestnuts and peas; lupines, nowadays usually a fodder plant, were also served as vegetables. Spices were essential in the Roman kitchen; there was a large variety of them, and the spice trade covered the entire ancient world. A favourite herb was silphium from Cyrenaica (now Libya), it was later called the 'compass plant' because it turns its young leaves north-south. For modern tastes silphium would be too pungent, though not as bad as the Persian gum resin asafoetida, which the Romans also liked, it smells somewhat like garlic, only more unpleasantly as its name suggests. But it is still an ingredient of some Indian dishes. The most widely used Roman spices were pepper and cinnamon.

We know very well what the Romans ate and how they cooked because a number of their cookery books have been preserved. The most famous of them is an encyclopaedia of the whole field of cooking, with hundreds of recipes collected by a gourmet called Apicius in the first century A.D., plus additions by cookery experts of the later imperial period.

Food in Old England

It would be wrong to assume that before the Roman invasion England was the ancient world's backwater, isolated from the civilized countries of the south and east. In fact, there was much trade going on; England had raw materials like tin and copper to export and wanted imports of various kinds, including spices, herbs, and wines. But the people were in general simple in their tastes and almost austere in their eating habits; it was a farming country where the inhabitants ate what they produced. There was much meat, milk, cheese, and fish in coastal regions; there was never any shortage of bread, or of beer, the Briton's daily drink.

Early farming

Of course the Romans, who stayed on the island for four hundred years, raised England's standard of living considerably. They organized the draining of marshes, the irrigation of farmland and its treatment with manure and sand; fruit and vegetables were planted. The Romans brought in new plants and animals. On the whole, the colonial officers and officials who built their villas and farmed their estates in Britain managed to eat as well as they had done at home, though there were no luxurious banquets in the imperial Roman style — the 'natives' as well as the legionaries stationed in the colony, who had to live on frugal rations, would have taken such extravagance amiss.

For the Britons the cuisine of their new masters was something of a revelation. All kinds of fowl were bred for food and served with spicy sauces; eggs were used in the kitchen for various dishes; there were fruit confections, cheese made with rennet, stews cooked with wheat-starch thickener; pepper in every savoury dish was the Roman cooks' overriding rule. Probably a number of mechanical devices such as the 'quern', a hand-turned flour mill, were also new to the Britons; they learnt the craft of preserving fruit; and they were shown how to cook with wine. However, the Romans could do little for the improvement of the English-grown wine which they found too sour for their taste — but so did many Britons themselves, who welcomed the increased import of wine from the south by the Romans.

The army of occupation needed a lot of bread, and new kinds of cereals were cultivated by the Romans to speed up supplies for the soldiers. A system of canals was created for shipping provisions as far as York. The Romans preferred wheat bread and liked wheat cakes; so they ordered the extensive growing of that cereal which so far had been neglected by the Britons. The result was, in the long run, that Britain became one of the major wheat-growing countries of the Western Hemisphere.

When the Romans left, the Britons were exposed to raids, invasions, and occupations by Saxons and Picts, Angles and Scots, Norsemen and Jutes. Most of what England had taken over from Roman civilized life vanished. Food was more than ever a matter of sheer survival, and there was much starvation. Often the invading tribes plundered the farms for their own coarse and noisy feasts. What had been a well-organized colony with long distance roads and canals and regular shipping connections with the Continent deteriorated into isolated patches of native and foreign settlements ruled by chieftains and self-styled kings, fighting each other most of the time. The Roman towns and trade centres had decayed, and the invaders imposed their unrefined way of life on the Britons who had stayed on; but many were withdrawing to the west, to Wales and Cornwall. Language, religion, farming systems, eating habits varied greatly in Kent and Northumbria, Wessex and Cumbria, Strathclyde and Mercia.

We know little of the internal history and the customs of these regions before their conversion to the Christian faith in the sixth and seventh centuries, but it seems that the people's chief concern was with the small wars that were being fought, and which made the development of wider agricultural areas impossible. Even after the establishing of Christian kingdoms the fighting and the rivalry went on until the framework of a united England began to emerge in the ninth century under Egbert of Wessex (and that of a united Scotland at the same time under Kenneth MacAlpine). Then the Danish invasion began on a large scale, and for some decades the Danes were the rulers in the greater part of England.

It was only with the Norman Conquest that the West Saxons, Mercians and Danes were unified into an English nation, for all England was conquered territory to the triumphant William and all land belonged to him.

This change of government probably made little difference to the daily lives of the common people at first, especially the peasants, but society was gradually transformed as the Norman feudal system was introduced. The aristocracy were almost all French, bound in service to the King and bound to provide a fighting force from their area in times of war: for which they were rewarded by being tenants-in-chief of a region. They in turn had followers whom they had to reward and sometimes maintained household knights with which to provide their quota for the feudal army. As lords of the manor these barons changed rural England into medieval feudal society.

At the bottom of this social structure was the class of 'Villeins', or serfs; the food-producing peasants tied to the lord's estate. Each of them had a small piece of land near his village and a share in the grazing and woodlands jointly used by the community. The lord charged the peasants rents in kind, taking from them much of their produce: grain, pigs, poultry, eggs, milk; even cattle had to be supplied for the lord's household instead of being sold in the nearest market. If the peasants were behind with their 'rent', the lord took it by force; part of their dues frequently consisted of the villeins' labour on his land, two or three days a week, and up to six at harvest time. To be sure, there were Courts of Law where the peasants could seek 'justice' in their controversies with the lord; but as he was the mightiest man in the district, and as a rule, himself the local magistrate, they had little chance of winning a court case against him.

Throughout most of the Middle Ages, the peasants lived mainly on coarse black bread; they had it for breakfast with some home-brewed ale, for their midday meal with butter and cheese or eggs, and for supper with bacon or sometimes meat, fresh in summer, salted in winter; on Fridays it was usually fish. Monasteries in inland areas often had a fish pond for this purpose. For the poor people, the main dish was usually gruel or vegetable soup. In short, the peasants existed largely on what they produced themselves, apart from salt which they had to buy in the market. What their food was like when the harvest had been poor has been vividly described by the fourteenth-century poet William Langland in his *Piers the Plowman:* —

> 'I haven't a penny,' said Piers, 'to pay for a pullet,
> nor for pork or for goose, but two green cheeses,
> a few curds and some cream and an oatmeal cake,
> and two loaves of bean and bran, baking for my children.
> By my soul, I say, I have no salt bacon,
> nor, by Christ, a kitchen boy for cooking a stew . . .'

Twenty years after Langland wrote his poem, the peasants of Kent and Essex rose under Wat Tyler's leadership, encouraged by the valiant priest John Ball. For nine days they controlled the kingdom until they were beaten by King Richard II's forces and Tyler was slain at Smithfield. Though the immediate cause of the rising was the enforcement of the Poll Tax, what made the peasants take up arms was their whole miserable existence as the underdogs of English society.

In the towns, the workmen and the artisans were much better off than the country people. Most important, they were free, they could to some extent bargain with their employers or customers for their rewards; there were markets where the housewives found a good selection of meats, poultry, dairy products, fruit and vegetables. When a workman's earnings were reasonably good he had his three meals a day, one of them perhaps eaten at a tavern. There were also public cookshops — the medieval forerunners of our modern 'take-away' shops — where roast and boiled meats, fish and poultry were always ready, as well as game when in season. Cold meat was often eaten at supper, and ale or wine was drunk by all townsmen except the very poorest.

Still, social distinctions were sharp, and there was not yet a large middle class. In the Middle Ages, the rich in town and country — the noblemen, the lords of the manors, the church dignitaries — ate lavishly and with much ceremony; banquets lasted for many hours. Several main courses were served, each of them consisting of a number of dishes. Every guest had before him a thick slice of bread on which the meat, up to half a dozen different kinds, was served; the gravy ran into the bread, which was thrown to the dogs or collected for the poor after the meal. that was the only way the people at the top of society remembered those at the bottom while they were feasting. A single item of the meal was 'produced' by the hosts and guests themselves — game; hunting was the only outdoor exercise they had, and it helped them to work up the healthy appetite they needed for their dinners. Commoners were not allowed to hunt; poachers who were caught were blinded or mutilated.

The wine that grew in England — largely cultivated by the monasteries — was not always good enough for the upper class; they preferred the red wine imported from France and the white wine from the Rhineland, spiced hippocras from Portugal, malmsey from Cyprus. But home-brewed ale was drunk by rich and poor alike.

As the Middle Ages were drawing to an end, the Church forgot more and more about its essential spiritual role and social duties; leading churchmen lived as extravagantly as the Court. For the enthronement feast of the Archbishop of York in 1467 one thousand sheep, 400 swans, over 300 pigs and as many calves, more than 100 oxen, 100 tons of wine and 300 tons of ale were supplied. Seventy-five years later, the first Archbishop of Canterbury after the English Reformation, Cranmer, issued an order that an Archbishop's dinner should not consist of more than six meat dishes, followed by only four 'second' dishes. The lower ranks of churchmen had to make do with three meat and two 'second' dishes.

The famous 'sirloin' story, however — that Henry VIII knighted a beef joint because of its supreme qualities — is no more than a popular legend. The word sirloin was a corruption of the French butcher's term *sur longe,* 'above the loin'.

A very far-reaching food revolution spread over Europe when a new historical age began with events which, at first, seemed only remotely connected with food — the discovery of hitherto unknown lands beyond the Atlantic Ocean.

2

FOOD ON THE MOVE

Why Columbus discovered America

The Egyptian and Roman cooks had developed the art of flavouring dishes with spices and condiments. In the early Middle Ages, however, European cooking coarsened again. The poor man's main concern was to get enough to eat, and the rich preferred quantity to quality: reading one of the medieval monster menus one gets the distinct impression that such banquets were not meant to be fun for the guests, but publicity for the hosts — demonstrations of their wealth and power.

But it was a small world, at least in Europe, with local rulers, markets and trading connections. The magnificent roads built by the Romans had crumbled to dust, their long-distance shipping routes disappeared and ships were built for war, not for carrying eastern spices to the west. The only condiment in constant demand was salt because of its preservative qualities, and throughout the European continent salt mining and trading retained and increased their age-old importance.

It was only in the twelfth century, when the scions of European nobility returned from their first crusades to the Middle East, that spices came into fashion again. The young warriors had not only sampled such exotic delicacies as dates and figs, melons and pomegranates — they had also developed a taste for the highly spiced food of the Orient. As usual in history, trade followed conquest, and European cooking acquired a new dimension: food became attractive again.

The Venetians had the ships for the revived spice trade available and cornered the market in pepper and cinnamon, ginger and galingale, cardamom and cumin, mace and cloves. Much of it came from Arabian ports, but before long the spice ships ventured further east, to India, to Indo-China, and eventually to China.

In the City of London, a Guild of Pepperers was founded to organize the spice trade; later it became the monopoly of the Guild of Grocers. In citizens' homes, housewives kept their expensive spices locked away. One of the delicacies they began to treasure was cane sugar from India, dear but much more practical for kitchen use than honey; until then the only sweetening agent. The production of sugar from white beet began in Europe only in the eighteenth century.

Spices, a matter of course in today's kitchens, played an enormous part not only in late-medieval cooking but in the countries' economies, in politics, in people's imaginations. Spices were also supposed to be invested with magical and medicinal powers; their taste and scent allured Europeans and suggested uses well beyond the purpose of improving dishes and disguising unwanted tang. A fifteenth-century German emperor, for instance, was said to have had his concubines rubbed with various spices such as tarragon or coriander, picking for his pleasure the one whose aroma happened to attract him that particular night. Among the members of the Italian Borgia family and their hangers-on, however, there was quite a fear of spices because they were sometimes used to cover the taste of poison, administered on the master's or mistress's orders by the chief spicer of that noble household.

When the Ottoman Turks had occupied the Balkan peninsula and conquered Constantinople in the fifteenth century, the end of the spice trade in the Middle East seemed to have come; the traditional routes between Europe and the Far East were blocked. The question was whether there was not a short-cut by sea to India and Indochina. If what an increasing number of 'natural philosophers' were saying (despite the danger of being burnt at the stake by the Inquisition) was true: that the earth was not a flat disc but a sphere — then the Indies might be reached by sailing westwards across the Atlantic. But no seafarer had yet put that theory to the test; it was, after all, a dreadful risk.

An experienced Genoese navigator, Christopher Columbus, was, nevertheless, prepared to take that risk. He suggested such an expedition in search of a western sea route to the spice countries to the King of Portugal and to Henry VII of England, but found no support. In the end it was Queen Isabella of Castile who, with the financial backing of a business-minded nobleman, agreed to put up the money. Apart from spices, both the Queen and the navigator also hoped to find gold, the metal everybody craved. In August, 1492, Columbus set out from Spain with three ships; the *Santa Maria* of 100 tons and two caravels of 50 and 40 tons —

ridiculously small for such a voyage by modern standards.

Ten weeks later he landed on an island which he believed to be part of the East Indian archipelago. But instead of the rich cities he had expected to find, there were only some settlements of a 'gentle, peaceful and simple people' who gave the sailors provisions in exchange for glass beads, which they hung around their necks. There were no spices, there was no gold on San Salvador, as he called that 'West Indian' island. Later he discovered Haiti, where he found some wild-growing spice plants which, he thought, could be perfected by cultivation. It was, from his point of view, a meagre result, apart from proving that the earth was indeed round. Further expeditions to the islands and to the mainland of America (as it was eventually called after Columbus' successor, Amerigo Vespucci) were just as disappointing.

The Portuguese explorer Vasco da Gama was luckier. By 1497, he had found the direct, though rather long, westward passage to India and its spices. Thanks to him, the Portuguese enjoyed a virtual spice-trade monopoly throughout the sixteenth century. Meanwhile, however, the new American territories — usurped as colonies by the Christian nations — were developing on rather unexpected lines, filling their new masters' coffers and larders with more riches than even the most prosperous spice trade could have yielded. Sadly the conquerors' methods were anything but Christian.

Luxuries from Slave Labour
While the Spanish *conquistadores* went on their predatory and genocidal expeditions through Central and South America in a frantic search for gold, the Dutch, the French, and the British preferred to establish permanent settlements. Spices were soon forgotten. Instead, the colonists found fascinating new foodstuffs which were to become of major importance not only in Europe. Some of them were made to 'migrate' to colonies in other parts of the world; in exchange, plants which promised profitiable cultivation were brought from Asia and Africa to America.

Plantations need workers, masses of them. Yet the native 'Indians' in America were too weak for hard labour. The African negroes, on the other hand, seemed well suited for it. The slave trade began.

In this abominable business, half a dozen civilized, Christian European countries have had the blackest of records; what they did has caused social, national, and international problems which are still besetting the world. Perhaps the Arabs who, as soon as they appeared on the 'Black Continent' in the eighth century, began to capture, transport, and sell Africans as slaves, gave the Europeans the idea. At any rate, the Portuguese had rapidly started the business already half a century before the discovery of America, capturing Negroes on their very first African expedition and bringing them home as slave workers. By 1492, they were doing this at an annual rate of a thousand men and women.

Ten years later, the Spanish were the first to ship African slaves to the West Indies and sell them there. Another twenty years later, African slaves were carrying the supplies for Cortez' and Pizarro's expeditions; they had been bought from Portuguese traders, for all Africa had been allocated to Portugal by the Pope. Needless to say, the other Christian nations took little notice of the Holy Father's decision, and a wild rivalry for slaves began all along the western coasts of Africa.

But the European traders did not take all the slaves they wanted by force of arms. Many tribal chiefs cooperated willingly, selling or bartering their own people for transport to the American colonies; they even raided neighbouring territories, kidnapping men and women for the traders. The demand was enormous, and the Portuguese were, of course, unable to prevent the other Europeans from muscling in. It was a free-for-all business. The Dutch West India Company did not hesitate to provide African manpower for the colonies of Holland's arch enemy, Spain. The French and the British, both of whom had wrested a number of West Indian islands from the Spanish, took up slave-trading in earnest in the middle of the seventeenth century. When Spain banned the trade for a short while and prices for slaves consequently went up, a golden age of slave-smuggling began. Buccaneers roamed the high seas and captured slave-carrying ships. Even the Germans, the Russians, and the Swedes took part — nations whose ships had until then rarely sailed the Atlantic.

The conditions under which the Africans were carried for five or more weeks to the West Indies or the American mainland were inhuman. Often chained to one another, with so little room that many had to lie in their neighbours' laps in 'kennels' 60 cm high, they were liable to fall ill of all kinds of diseases; there were epidemics of dysentery, smallpox, eye infections, and even a few outbreaks of plague. As many as half of each ship load of slaves did not survive the journey. The crews were also prone to catch the slaves' diseases, and their death rate was not much lower. Slave riots were put down savagely; there would have been many more had the traders not taken the precaution of assembling their human freight from various tribes with different languages so that the slaves could not speak — and plot — in larger groups; they had to learn their masters' language in due course to communicate among themselves.

A West Indian sugar plantation (Radio Times Hulton Picture Library)

By how many souls was Africa depleted during the three-and-a-half centuries of the slave trade? It has been estimated that during the first 100 years of colonization (up to 1600) one million blacks were shipped to the West Indies, North and South America. A further 1,750,000 followed in the seventeenth century, and nearly four million in the eighteenth. The nineteenth century saw a sharp reduction of the trade as the conscience of the European nations, particularly Britain's, awoke at last, and governments were forced to outlaw the whole horrid business. A total of seven million enslaved and transported Africans has been estimated for the whole period from the discovery of the New World to the abolition of slavery by the United States in the 1860s. As the practice of slaving ceased, that of colonizing Africa by the European nations began, and by the end of the last century practically the whole of the African continent was split up into European colonies and spheres of influence. No wonder that Africa's unhappy history has made it a constant source of trouble and unrest in our time, and that the now independent African states find it difficult to advance on the road to democracy from which they had been barred so long by European greed and callousness.

The first great incentive for the slave trade was cane sugar from the West Indies — not only because European housewives and cooks wanted it but also because of its highly desirable by-product, rum. Early in the eighteenth century, rum was introduced as a 'naval ration' on British ships, and in the 1770s Captain Cook, who discovered Australia, set the example of mixing the sailors' 'grog' with lime, orange, or lemon juice to combat scurvy. Naval officers had found out, purely by experience, that the remedy for that debilitating illness lay in citrus fruit juice. It was only in our own century that the enormous importance of vitamins for the human body was discovered (see Chapter 4); a deficiency of vitamin C — ascorbic acid — was the cause of scurvy on long sea journeys

A major reason for the rapidly mounting demand for sugar from the slave plantations in the West Indies was the introduction of three new beverages in Europe: cocoa, coffee and tea; all of which needed sugar. Columbus had first brought cocoa beans from America, where the plant grew wild, but in Spain no one knew what to do with it. Twenty-five years later, Cortez reported that the Mexican Aztecs drank large quantites of an infusion made from roasted and ground cocoa beans, which they called *chocolatl*. For a century, the Spanish kept the recipe for chocolate a closely guarded secret, but somehow the French learnt it, and the aristocracy adopted it as a luxury drink and in the form of solid sweetmeats. It was a Frenchman who opened London's first 'chocolate house' in Bishopsgate in the middle of the seventeenth century. Within a decade or two, such establishments sprang up all over the metropolis; one of them, White's in St. James, became England's first club. It was a meeting-place for the most reckless wealthy gamblers.

Coffee originated in Ethiopia but remained unknown outside that country until the fifteenth century, when it was introduced in Arabia. Two hundred years later it set out from there on a curious voyage around the world. A burgomaster of Amsterdam, who traded with the East, took some coffee plants from the port of Mocha, in the Yemen, to Batavia in Java, where the Dutch settlers started coffee-farming on a large scale; from there, the

French took the plant to their colony Martinique in the West Indies. Eventually it was Jamaica and Brazil which became Europe's main coffee suppliers, thanks to the black slaves.

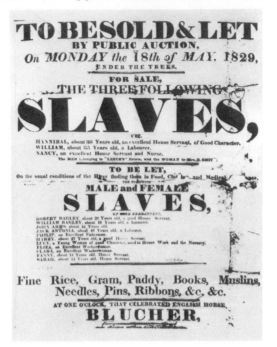

A Jamaican poster for a sale of slaves, bearing a date twenty-two years after Britain had forbidden any further importation of slaves, but seven years before slavery itself had been finally abolished.

Chocolate had conquered the *salons* of Europe as an upper-class ladies' drink. However, right from the start, coffee was a man's beverage, to be drunk, like wine, in good company. From the middle of the seventeenth century, coffee-houses opened in London by their hundreds (though the first one in England was established in Oxford). Their attraction was that they developed into rendezvous of people with similar professional or business interests, cultural leanings or political opinions. The writers, the clergy, the army stalwarts, the artists — they all had their favourite coffee-houses. One of them, run by a Welshman called Lloyd, was the meeting-place of men with shipping interests, and it was here that the world's most famous insurance company was founded; it still bears that Welshman's name. In 1675, Charles II tried — without success — to close down the coffee-houses as hotbeds of political conspiracy.

32

A London coffee-house in the 18th century

Tea, Tobacco, Turkeys, and Tomatoes

By 1715, when London was said to have well over two thousand coffee-houses, the third of the new beverages was already on its way. Probably its earliest mention in print had been in 1658, when the *Mercurius Politicus,* a London journal, carried this advertisement:—

> That Excellent, and by all Physicians approved, China drink, called by the Chineans Tcha, by other nations Tay alias Tea, is sold at the Sultaness Head Cophee-House.

It was a gross overstatement that 'all physicians' approved of tea, for few of them had ever heard of it at the time. Even London's conscientious chronicler Pepys, who was interested in anything new, had his first cup of tea only in 1660. That was also the year of the Restoration — and of the first tax on tea to keep King and Government in funds. Thus it started its career in England as a treat only for the wealthy. It was already expensive when it arrived, having been shipped all the way from China where it had been a national drink since the seventh century A.D. Before England made its acquaintance it had already been introduced in Russia, Germany, Holland, and Portugal, not only from China, but also from Japan.

*An Indian tea picker. Inset shows what is actually picked —
two leaves and a bud.*

At the beginning of the eighteenth century, 10,000 kilograms of China tea were imported annually in Britain — at its end the figure was 10 million kilograms, and the price had dropped considerably, thanks to the smugglers. No less than three quarters of all the tea drunk by the British was smuggled in and sold at cut-price. Tea had by this time ousted coffee almost completely as a popular drink, so much so that the American-born scientist and statesman Count Rumford (more about him near the end of this chapter) tried to revive the drinking of coffee in preference to 'that miserable and unwholesome wash which the poor people in England drink under the name of tea!' Needless to say, Rumford failed with his campaign.

Tea had become a social factor, and at least once it made a forceful foray into politics. The English settlers who emigrated to the North American colonies took the tea-drinking habit with them, and they were infuriated when the British Parliament passed laws favouring the London-based East India Company as tea importers at the expense of the Massachusetts traders. The result was the famous 'Boston Tea Party' of 1773, generally regarded as one of the loudest opening shots of the American War of Independence: settlers disguised as Red Indians threw 342 chests of tea, which arrived soon after that legislation, overboard as an act of defiance.

However, the great era of England's tea-drinking was still to come. It began as late as 1839, when the first shipment of Indian tea was brought to London from Assam, where botanists had found wild-growing tea bushes. Tea plantations were started in Assam on a large scale; Ceylon (now Sri Lanka) followed only in the late 1870s, but quickly developed into one of the major tea-producing countries.

By the turn of the century, Indian/Ceylonese tea had all but ousted Chinese tea from popular favour in England, not only because of its unsophisticated taste but mainly because it was cheaper due to the shorter journey from India/Ceylon. Today, more than one third of all the tea exported by the producer countries is consumed in Britain.

There is still some historical dissent about the introduction of tobacco in Europe, from where its use spread to the rest of the world. It was, in fact, Columbus' interpreter, Luis de Torres, who saw the first New World inhabitants smoke in Cuba, and took some tobacco leaves back to Spain. Columbus, however, regarded the matter as so unimportant that he never included it in his reports. Other explorers found that the West Indies used tobacco as a medicine and in religious ceremonies, inhaling smoke from the smouldering, dried leaves through a forked, hollow cane which they called *tobago*. A Spanish court physician brought another batch of leaves back from Mexico in 1559, and then the Spanish courtiers began to smoke. The habit spread to Lisbon, where the French ambassador, Jean Nicot, picked up some leaves to take them to Paris — and the French court, too, started smoking. His name has been preserved by the term for the poisonous alcaloid in the plant, nicotine.

Sailors returning from America brought tobacco leaves to England; but Sir Walter Raleigh, who is usually but wrongly credited with the discovery, was merely the man who made smoking fashionable at the English Court in the 1560s. Within half a century, smoking — at first believed to cure all sorts of ailments — had become a habit among English men and women of all classes, despite various attempts to stamp it out by laws, punishment, heavy import duties and even excommunication by the Church. Originally, tobacco was used in pipes and in the form of tightly rolled leaves which the Spanish called *cigarros;* it was only during the Crimean War that cigarettes, a Russian invention, were adopted by British soldiers. Until this day, the constant warnings of the dangers of smoking by the medical profession have had only a limited effect among the addicts.

A Dutch pipe smoker of the early 17th century

Staple Foods

A great migration of foodstuffs began with the exploration and colonization of the Americas. One of the first discoveries made by the English settlers on the North American east coast was a large, wild bird which — for reasons that are still something of a mystery — they called 'turkey'. It became a popular meal in Europe and in America itself, where the colonists started the tradition of cooking it for their Christmas dinner.

The list of foods, and particularly of food plants, which America gave to the rest of the world is immense. There were many kinds of fruit and vegetables which contributed to the variety of European meals: pineapples and tomatoes, 'french' beans and scarlet runners, red and green peppers, pumpkins and avocado pears, peanuts and vanilla. The newcomers in America had to learn from the natives how to prepare and use these unfamiliar foodstuffs. Their seeds and plants were also shipped eastwards across the Atlantic, but it took a long time of experimenting until Europeans found out which of them would grow, and where.

Europe's staple food had been bread baked from wheat and rye. In all countries, at the rich man's and the poor man's table, bread accompanied every savoury dish, and for the poorest the proverbial crust of bread *was* their meal. In Asia, rice has been the staple food in most areas for so long that the beginnings of its cultivation are shrouded in the mists of pre-history; all we know is that rice was grown and eaten in Siam (Thailand) in the fourth millenium B.C. and in China in the third, though perhaps only south of the Yangtse river. Northern China and India became rice areas probably during the second millenium B.C., with Japan following suit. In the Middle Ages, the Arabs brought rice cultivation to Spain. Today, Italy is the only European country to grow it. However, her major staple food is now 'pasta'.

How this came about is uncertain, but it could not have happened before the latter part of the Middle Ages. The most popular version of the noodle story is that Marco Polo brought the idea back from China around 1300. But it is more likely that the Chinese noodle, having reached the Middle East via India, was brought to Venice by Arab traders before Marco Polo's time. It seemed a great idea to the Italians with their wealth of wheat — though, oddly enough, they called the novelty 'macaroni' after the Greek work for barley. Somewhat later, a thinner version was introduced by the pasta-makers; it was called 'spaghetti', from *spage*, which means string. By the beginning of the sixteenth century, pasta was strongly competing with bread and rice as

Italy's staple food, and by the eighteenth, macaroni and spaghetti had won the battle.

Spain, Portugal, and Italy welcomed Columbus' discovery of maize, or 'Indian corn', from which the native women made flour for bread. The fast growth of this cereal astounded the early settlers in America — it had been forgotten that already in antiquity maize had been cultivated in the eastern parts of the Roman Empire. The rediscovered cereal was widely accepted as a new staple food, but where it was consumed without much vitamin-rich meat, fruit and vegetables, people's health suffered from the deficiency disease pellagra, which begins with a sunburn-like skin ailment and may end up with mental disorder. This made maize fall out of popular favour in many areas of southern Europe, though the Italian porridge-type *polenta,* made from maize flour, is still a poor man's dish in some regions; it was also accepted in Africa as a subsistence food.

Another American discovery that went to Africa was manioc, or cassava, the source of the starchy substance tapioca. It was first found in Haiti, the European colonizers brought it to Africa, where it is greatly in favour with many tribes. Groundnuts, pineapples, french beans, and papaya or pawpaw were also brought from the tropical climate of Central America to that of Africa for cultivation. Thus the Europeans, who did such immense harm to the Dark Continent, also helped to ease its food problems. Parts of Asia, too, gladly accepted some American fruits and vegetables — while Indian curries were improved, and made even 'hotter', by chilli peppers brought over from Mexico.

As a return gift for the new foodstuffs it received from the New World, Africa gave the yam to America: a tropical climbing plant with edible tubers, which is often thought to be the same as the American-born 'sweet potato' (called *batata* by the West Indians), also with edible tubers ('with a taste reminiscent of chestnuts', as the European discoverers described it). Botanically, however, the yam and the sweet potato belong to different families. The yam was sent over with the slave ships because the Africans were used to it as one of their staple foods. Yams, rice, and bananas from Asia were all made to grow in the West Indies and tropical parts of the American mainland.

The sweet potato is no close relation to *the* potato either. How this most important American food plant was introduced in Europe, and eventually accepted by it, and what part it has played in European affairs is quite a dramatic chapter in the history of food.

The Potato Story

The popular version of the first appearance of the potato in the Old World is that Sir Walter Raleigh and/or Sir Francis Drake brought it from America to England at the end of the sixteenth century. In fact it was one of Pizarro's officers who took it back to Spain more than fifty years earlier, from Peru; where it had been cultivated for no less than 4500 years. Some of the tubers were sent to the Pope, and from the Vatican they found their way to a famous Walloon botanist, who advocated the introduction of the potato as it was a hardy edible plant, well suited to the European soil. His suggestion was taken up first in Holland. Doctors recommended the new foodstuff on various grounds — it was 'very substantial, good and restorative, though somewhat windy'; it stopped 'fluxes of the bowels'; and it 'cured consumption'. The best ways to prepare it were to boil, bake, or roast it and eat it with butter and salt, or with orange or lemon juice. Some savants declared that the potato 'increases seed and provokes lust, causing fruitfulness in both sexes'.

Yet the general public took an instant dislike to it. Vegetables were not yet regarded as healthy and necessary ingredients of a meal, and this one seemed rather suspicious: it was the first edible plant to be grown not from seed but from tubers, and it was also 'abnormal' because it had underground stems producing more tubers, which were supposed to be the edible part of the plant. Some people thought this was a misunderstanding; they cooked and ate the leaves and promptly became sick. John Gerarde, the great English herbalist, planted potato tubers from America in his garden in Holborn in 1596, and recorded that they grew and prospered there 'as in their own native country'. In that very year, England had a catastrophic famine, but Gerarde was unable to make even the hungry poor of London try his potatoes.

Gardeners and farmers in various parts of the Continent also planted potatoes, but reactions against them were as frequent as they were absurd. Already in 1619, potatoes were banned in Burgundy as they 'might cause leprosy'. In Switzerland people believed that eating too many of them would produce scrofula. In Prussia there was little early resistance to the potato — the authorities demanded its cultivation and the peasants obeyed. But in 1774, there was a famine in Pomerania, and Frederick the Great sent the citizens of Kolberg some cart-loads of potatoes; to the King's anger they wouldn't touch them, hungry as they were.

Six years later, the aversion to potatoes in Central Europe

reached its climax. The War of the Bavarian Succession between Frederick and Austria became known as the 'potato war' because both armies, facing each other in Bohemia, were conducting an indecisive and protracted campaign on insufficient provisions and had to feed themselves by raiding the farmlands in the area. All they got were potatoes, which they dug out of the fields. When there were none left the war ended, but the bitter memories lingered on. The result was the soldiers' lifelong hatred of potatoes, and the peasants' refusal to plant any more, especially in Bavaria where they did not want to run the same risks as their Bohemian friends.

Count Rumford as a British Colonel in 1783

The man who succeeded in breaking down the general dislike of the potato and the prejudice against it in Bavaria, and eventually in other continental countries, was the (already mentioned) Count Rumford; an American who gained great fame and influence in Central Europe as well as in England. He was one of the unique characters which the late eighteenth century produced — arrogant and selfish, authoritarian in his attitude to people, but surprisingly progressive as a social innovator and brilliant as a scientist. Born Benjamin Thompson, a New England farmer's son, he married a rich widow and acted as a spy for the British among his rebellious compatriots during their struggle for independence. He had to escape to England, where he was given a Government post, and in 1784 he accepted an invitation by the Elector of Bavaria to look around that country and suggest some reforms.

The Elector got much more than he had bargained for. Thompson studied the Bavarian scene for four years, working out a whole scheme of radical reforms which started with Bavaria's Holy Cow, the army. He knew that he risked the Elector's wrath; but instead of the Order of the Boot he got the post of Minister of War and Police, with *carte blanche* to do with the army what he liked. Never before had a foreigner been given a position of so much trust and power by any German ruler.

In fact, what Thompson did was to create Europe's first people's army by making the soldiers citizens, and the citizens soldiers — better paid, clothed, housed, taught, occupied, entertained than any army had ever been. And in particular: better fed. He was the first administrator to study food problems from the biological and medical as well as from the economic and organizational angles.

In Thompson's scheme, each garrison was directed to lay out its own 'military garden' to provide the soldiers with vegetables; and this was where the potato came in. He recognized it as the ideal staple food for large groups of the population such as garrisoned soldiers and urban workers in an age of intensifying industrialization. Completely ignoring the general aversion to the potato he ordered patches for seeding them to be laid out in all garrison gardens; each allotment was put under the care of an individual soldier who came from the land, to get the future farmers acquainted with the potato and encourage them to plant it on their own farms when they returned home.

And lo and behold — the potato was a great success. Within a few years the Bavarians accepted it as their new staple food, especially in the form of dumplings. The Bavarian example helped greatly to make the potato at last popular as a cheap, energy-sustaining, and weather-resistant food plant in the new industrial areas that were developing all over Central and Western Europe.

Thompson also employed the army for turning a wild, marshy

stretch of land along Munich's river, the Isar, into a beautiful park for the citizens; it was called *Englischer Garten* because he took his cue from London's Hyde Park. The grateful Elector created him a Count, and he chose as his new name that of the American town where his rise in society had begun with a profitable marriage — Rumford (now Concord).

The Potato Famine in Ireland, 1846. Starving peasants at the gate of a workhouse. (Radio Times Hulton Picture Library)

Another highly successful scheme of his was the elimination of beggary in Munich in 1790. On New Year's Day — the traditional date of alms-giving — he had most of the 3000 beggars who made the streets of the Bavarian capital unsafe seized by the army. They were invited to come to a workhouse he had fitted with workshops for various trades with clean, warm rooms, and with a splendidly equipped kitchen; scientifically designed by himself. He had also created the recipe of a standard dish; a nourishing soup with potatoes as one of the main ingredients. It is still well known in Bavaria under the name of *Rumfordsuppe*. After some initial resistance the beggars-turned-workers began to like it.

Rumford was the creator of domestic science. He designed an economical kitchen range which was eventually adopted all over the Continent and in Britain. After settling again in London he invented a non-smoking fireplace which was generally used throughout the nineteenth and well into our own century (though in his own home in South Kensington he had London's first

42

central-heating system installed); and he founded the Royal Institution as a pioneer establishment for scientific research and teaching. He picked a young Cornishman, Humphry Davy, as a lecturer, and Davy in his turn chose Michael Faraday as his assistant.

There was one ghastly episode in the history of the potato in Europe. Since the 1580s, 'Ireland's lazy root' had been cultivated; gradually replacing bread as the nutritional mainstay to such an extent that Karl Marx' friend, Friedrich Engels, wrote in 1844: 'On the lowest ground of the (social) ladder, among the Irish, potatoes form the sole food.' Two years later, the potato crop failed all over Ireland. In the famine which followed, tens of thousands of people died, and well over half a million emigrated to America within a decade. Some historians say that Ireland has not yet recovered from the long-term effects of that catastrophe.

3

FOOD AND POLITICS

Britain's Agricultural Revolution
We have to take another look at the Middle Ages because there were, during that period of apparent stagnation after the fall of the Roman Empire, some important developments in food history.

The period began with a great migration of peoples which kept Europe in a state of flux for several centuries. Tribes from the near and distant east suddenly appeared inside what had been the Roman Empire but was now no longer defended. The Franks and other Germanic tribes reached the Rhine and the Danube, Hungary was invaded by the Vandals (who later crossed to North Africa), and Dacia – now Romania – by the West Goths who kept pushing on, eventually occupying the Balkans and parts of Italy, including Rome. The East Goths, who had come down with their Teutonic western brothers from the Baltic, established their realm at the Black Sea; they were attacked by the Huns, but later the two peoples marched on together – to a terrible defeat at Châlons in France at the hands of the West Goths. The Huns, under their leader Attila, retreated to Hungary and eventually settled there; the East Goths dispersed after a few more military expeditions and another defeat in the sixth century.

During the later stages of these invasions and migrations, a few more tribes entered world history. They were the Angles, the Saxons and the Jutes, many of whom sought new homes where they would be safe from the 'Barbarians' from the east, and crossed over to England, and the Slavs, who had established their kingdom Wendonia, in what is now Eastern Germany and South-western Poland. They too marched west and extended their territory right to the gates of Hamburg.

What had caused that massive migration, that westward drift which completely changed the map of Europe? It must have been a fundamental transformation of the climate of northern Asia, i.e. Siberia. We are not sure what that climatic change was; it could have been droughts affecting the Siberian forests, causing the Asian tribes to move westwards and thereby pushing a wave of peoples before them. Most of the migrating tribes were still in the hunting stage, with little experience in agriculture; they were probably attracted by the fleshpots — and the comparative wealth — of western Europe.

But the Slavs, who came in the sixth century, were already a farming people, and they brought with them an innovation which was to have a powerful influence on European agriculture. It was a new heavyweight plough. Until then, the generally used implement of the peasant had been the scratch plough, no more than a hooked branch which turned the surface soil over. The effect was that the top soil soon became exhaused by superficial ploughing.

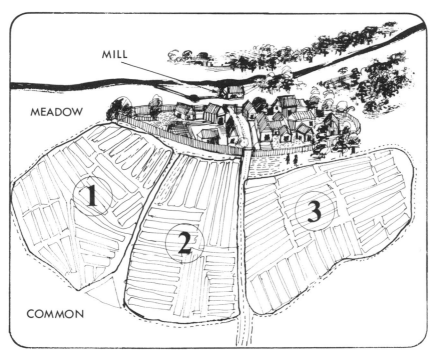

Medieval village and 3-field system

The Slavs' plough was much more efficient. It was a 'mouldboard' plough with a knife blade digging vertically into the soil, a plough-share which cut horizontally through it at grass-root

45

level, and a mouldboard which turned the earth clods over. By cutting deeper, and by its sheer weight, this implement not only worked more thoroughly, it also made it possible to cultivate virgin soil and wasteland which had until then remained untilled for lack of an efficient tool.

The new plough not only increased food production and, as a result, population; it also had a profound effect on the social structure of the regions where it was introduced, which gradually extended over most of Europe. A crooked branch had cost the peasant nothing, the heavyweight mouldboard plough had to be made by a craftsman, metal had to be mined for its construction, a blacksmith had to furnish the blades, and a team of oxen was needed to pull it. The big landowners could afford the expense, but the individual peasants could not. The obvious solution for the villagers was to club together for cultivating their land, sharing the expense of the plough and of a team of oxen to work it. The English system which developed in the Middle Ages meant that each peasant owned several strips of land of about one acre each, scattered around the village, seldom adjoining. But the villagers ploughed and reaped those strips together. Grazing land was commonly owned.

It was not an ideal system, yet it persisted for centuries. Farming could not make much progress under it; the individual peasant had no chance of introducing any improvements on his land — he had to keep doing what his neighbours did, conforming to the lowest common denominator. Agricultural reformers tried to persuade the farming communities to abolish the system, and eventually the 'Enclosure Movement' broke it down.

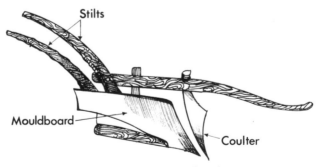

Mid-17th century plough

This movement, the essential part of what became known as Britain's Agricultural Revolution, was in fact the acceleration of a development which had already begun in Tudor times; by the

46

middle of the nineteenth century, it had changed practically the whole of the country's farming system. Gradually, each village was enclosed, or fenced off, the scattered open fields were abolished and the land redivided. Each farmer was allotted one solid block of land which he could cultivate as he pleased, independent from his neighbours, and which enabled him to carry out better, selective livestock breeding.

In most villages the people saw the need for a change, and understood that the new system was superior to the old. If the majority of farmers in an area agreed to introduce enclosure, Parliament was petitioned, an Enclosure Act for the village or region was passed, and a commission was appointed to decide which farmer should receive which block of land. During the first half of the eighteenth century, some 200 Enclosure Acts were passed, and between 1750 and 1850 there were thousands of them, affecting about 5½ million acres — nearly one fifth of all arable land.

But the new system had one serious drawback. The small farmers, unable to afford the husbandry of a large piece of land, were at a serious disadvantage. Most of them had to sell the strips of land they owned, and seek work as day labourers — or at the new factories in the cities. This was how the bulk of the labour force for the Industrial Revolution was recruited.

The era of the big agricultural producer began. It transformed the countryside; it increased the food supply greatly by various new methods, which could now be introduced on a large scale. The Enclosure Movement affected the country's economy as well as its social structure and people's eating habits no less than industrialization did.

While England was changing into a country of large farms, most Continental countries — especially France, Germany, and Italy — retained a great number of their small holdings well into the nineteenth century or even until today. But it would be wrong to assume that farming techniques made little progress in the Western Hemisphere until recent times, which brought mechanization to the land. In fact, one of the most important innovations began over a thousand years ago; or rather the revival of a very ancient system: crop rotation.

In antiquity, some of the Mediterranean peoples had found that the soil tended to become less fertile the longer it carried one particular crop, and a change of crop often restored its productivity. Leaving a field to lie fallow for a year or six months had been an even older system, as we know from the rules laid down in the Old Testament. The Romans did it, too: half the land was cultivated while the other half was left fallow. But it was the more intensive cultivation made possible by the introduction of the mouldboard plough and the formation of village communes which brought the crop rotation idea back, first in Charlemagne's empire and in England during the Saxon era. The arable land around the village was divided into three sectors: one under cereals, another under vegetable crops such as beans or peas, and the third remaining fallow until the next seed-time.

The three-field system did not only improve the food supply for humans, but also for an animal that was then beginning to take part in European farm life — the horse. Now it could be regularly provided with its proper fodder, oats, alternatively from one of the three fields. There was also a newly arrived invention — it had come all the way from China to Europe — which made working horses much happier and therefore more efficient: the collar harness, replacing the old neck strap which nearly choked the poor animal with every pull at a heavy load, constricting its windpipe. The horse also got a new type of nailed shoe which enabled it to work on moist fields and to get a good grip on country roads. Gradually, horses were replacing oxen as 'power units' for ploughing and transport work.

Selective breeding of animals and plants to improve their qualities is also mentioned in the Old Testament, but throughout antiquity and the Middle Ages breeding was never very efficient as it was hampered by an overgrowth of erroneous religious and superstitious notions. It was only in the eighteenth century that systematic animal breeding, coupled with new ideas about feeding, produced good results, especially in England — the Leicester sheep, for instance, combining meat and wool qualities, and the Durham short-horn cattle. Early in that century, the statesman and gentleman farmer Lord Townshend brought home some modern methods from Holland, where he had been Britain's emissary. He developed the Norfolk four-course crop rotation system; which included turnips and clover as animal fodder and eliminated the waste of the fallow field. At the same time, Jethro Tull, the first of a generation of scientific agricultural writers, invented a corn drill and a horsehoe for weeding between rows of seeds. England's population was growing fast, and more food was needed — a demand which was to increase more and more as the Industrial Revolution was getting into its stride at the end of the eighteenth century.

An invention which plays quite a large role in modern life,

48

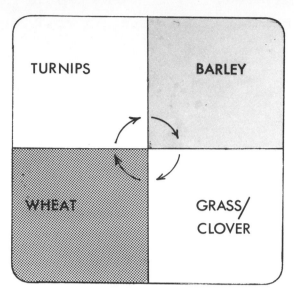

4-crop rotation system

though not an essential one, is ice cream. It seems to have been made, like so many others, by the Chinese, perhaps as long as five thousand years ago; bowls of natural snow, laced with fruit juice, were sold in the towns. Information about the Chinese speciality must have reached Alexander the Great of Macedonia in the fourth century before Christ, for the story goes that he sent his slaves to the mountains to gather hard-packed snow, which was then mixed with honey, milk, and fruit juice, to be served at banquets. But then the idea sank into oblivion until it was revived by the Italians in the first half of the sixteenth century. They collected ice and snow from the hills and added fruit juice for flavouring. Naturally, it had to be eaten before it melted; but it had a certain storage life in the 'ice houses' which the very rich had built in their deepest cellars.

Refrigeration as a means of preserving food was used already in the ice age, though the principle — killing the bacteria before they could make the food inedible — was, of course, unknown. Prehistoric man had plenty of natural ice at his disposal during that period, and he built primitive storage containers from stone and earth for keeping fish and meat for months in a bed of ice. Again, it was the Chinese who built the first deep ice houses in the eighth century B.C., using winter ice which kept food fresh for a limited period.

The underground ice houses which were dug in many European

49

castles and mansions of the wealthy aristocracy during the latter part of the Middle Ages were large, brick-lined chambers, two thirds of which were filled with ice in winter; in the upper third part, perishable foodstuffs were stored. They kept cool throughout the summer if the weather was not too hot. An outlet at the bottom of the chamber provided a gulley for the water. When Henry II of France married Catherine de Medici in 1533, her Italian cooks made a different kind of water ice for each day of the wedding celebrations, using the ice from the ice house in the palace cellar. The common people of London got their first taste of an iced drink in 1660, the year of the Restoration, when an ice house was built in St. James's Park, mainly for the preparation of sherbet, or sorbet, which was sold from stalls in the park.

Still, two centuries went by before ice cream became a truly popular delicacy. The first modern methods of refrigeration were developed in the second half of the nineteenth century (more about them later in this chapter), and in Central Europe as well as in England hordes of Italian ice-cream sellers appeared in the streets with their little barrows. The ices were home-made, but after the first World War their mass manufacture began in all the industrialized countries; eventually the motorized ice vans — now with their tape-recorded chimes — became a familiar sight in the streets. It is interesting to note that an earlier attempt to introduce an ice-cream-like sweet failed in America; around 1810, President Madison had frozen custard served at one of his official dinners, but the lady who took the first bite collapsed in a dead faint, and that was the end of the experiment.

But let us return to the end of the seventeenth century when London was treated to another culinary innovation, made by one of the most interesting personalities of the time. Denis Papin was a French Huguenot who had found refuge at the Pall Mall home of the famous physicist, Robert Boyle, with whom he worked on the pressure of gases; Papin's special field of research was steam, for he wanted to invent a steam engine.

In 1682, the two physicists invited the members of the Royal Society to a 'scientific supper' for the demonstration of Papin's 'bone digester', as he called his invention. It was a cooking machine which worked on the principle that when water or juice is boiled in a tightly closed vessel so that the steam cannot escape, the pressure increases so much that the steam is heated far beyond the boiling-point of water. The superheated steam helps to cook the food in the vessel much faster and more thoroughly than in an ordinary saucepan. 'I took beef bones that had never been

50

boiled, but kept dry a long time,' Papin wrote, 'and of the hardest part of the leg; these being put into a little glass pot, with water, and inserted into the engine.'

The meal was a great success. The toughest bones, reported one of the savants, were 'made as soft as cheese', and there was 'an incredible quantity of gravy' as well as a delicious beef jelly. Only 230 grammes of coal had been used. The cast-iron 'bone digester' with its tightly-fitting lid also included another invention of Papin's: a safety valve which opened when a weight was lifted by the steam pressure, to make sure that the vessel would not blow up. Today we know the modern version of Papin's 'bone digester' very well — we call it the pressure cooker. Yet he never achieved the invention of a steam engine and died, a penniless man, in the slums of London.

Hunger and Revolution

Since biblical times, sieges of towns had always meant that their inhabitants and the defending soldiers were cut off from food supplies, and many a fortified place had to surrender for sheer hunger. But it was Napoleon who first used the system of blockade in the hope of forcing a whole nation down on its knees. He called the decree he issued in 1806 the 'Continental System'. By this Great Britain was to be in a state of blockade, which meant that all commerce and communication with her was banned for France and her allies. A year later, Britain issued an Order in Council which decreed a similar ban in reverse: no British or neutral ship was to enter any port belonging to the French or their allies.

Neither blockade nor counter-blockade was very effective; as to Napoleon, he did not have the ships to enforce his ban, and even the British Navy was unable to put the entire French-dominated coast under siege. But the Continental System was the main cause of Napoleon's attack on Russia which openly refused to comply with his blockade decrees — and that invasion turned out to be the beginning of his end as the ruler of Europe. Besides, Napoleon himself discovered that France needed British goods no less than Britain needed Continental imports, and the double blockade fizzled out.

But it was an ill wind that brought some good to England: the blockade scared the country into intensifying her efforts to feed herself, especially as she was now in the middle of her Industrial Revolution which made increasing demands on food production and distribution. A new social class, the urban proletariat, had to be fed, and that cheaply: a challenge which had to be met by the Government, the landowners, and the industrialists, lest the same dreaded upheaval happened as in France in 1789.

The new farming methods, largely based on the enclosure reform, did indeed bring great increases in the food supply for Britain's growing population, which doubled in the short space of seventy years, from 1760 to 1830. Cheap grain, however, had to be imported, and the landowners grew worried. In 1815, Parliament yielded to their urgent demands, and enacted that foreign corn must not be imported until the home price of wheat was 80 shillings a quarter — a law that caused great alarm among the common people, for it meant that the price of bread was kept high. This was also in the interest of the industrialists, for high food prices made sure that their supply of workers did not dry up; hunger drove men and women (often enough with their children) to the factories and made them accept miserable wages.

In 1828 — when the Corn Laws were renewed for the first time — the German poet Heinrich Heine visited England. He wrote:—

> I have seen the greatest wonder which the world can show to the astonished spirit: I have seen it and am still astonished; and still there remains fixed in my memory the stone forest of houses, and amid them the rushing stream of faces of living men with all their motley passions, all their terrible impulses of love, of hunger, and of hatred.

Karl Marx and Friedrich Engels were convinced that the socialist revolution would come first in England where the living conditions of the proletariat seemed intolerable. Among the workers in the industrial towns, wrote Engels, 'we find the animal food reduced to a small bit of bacon cut up with the potatoes'; on a still lower level of existence, 'even this disappears, and there remains only bread, cheese, porridge, and potatoes'. There were hardly any fresh vegetables, fruit, milk, butter, or eggs in the proletarian diet, with the result that people suffered chronically from rickets, scurvy, anaemia, tooth and eye diseases, while life in the slums made tuberculosis widespread. Infantile mortality was extremely high, and many children who did survive failed to grow to normal size.

The working-class families that had come from the country had no more home-grown food; there was neither time nor space for home-baking or brewing, there were no pigs to slaughter, no cows to milk. They became dependent for all their food on shops; the quantities they could afford to buy were ridiculously small — tea was often sold by the ounce — and most families had to ask for credit for their bread and groceries, at least until the next payday, but many of them were in debt for their whole lives.

During a long working day in the factory there were, as a rule, only two short breaks for eating; some employers provided meagre meals for their workers, but they had to eat them at their machines. No wonder that men and women spent a good part of their small earnings, up to half of the money, on drink, mostly beer and gin. The pubs, of course, were warmer than their barely-heated homes,

GIN

George Cruikshank's cartoon of a nineteenth century 'gin palace', where many of the working class drowned the sorrows of their miserable existence in drink. (Mary Evans Picture Library)

and drinking among mates helped the workers to forget their wretched existence. What the 'hungry forties' of the nineteenth century were like has been vividly described by Disraeli, Mrs. Gaskell, and many other writers; especially Dickens. In his *Old Curiosity Shop* he paints the scene of rural England in the grip of the Industrial Revolution:—

> On every side, and as far as the eye could see into the heavy distance, tall chimneys crowding on each other poured out their plague of smoke, obscured the light, and made foul the melancholy air. On mounds of ashes by the wayside, sheltered only by a few rough boards or rotten pent-house roofs, strange engines spun and writhed like tortured creatures . . . Dismantled houses here and there appeared, tottering to earth, propped up by fragments of others that had fallen down, unroofed, windowless, blackened, desolate, but yet inhabited. Men, women, children, wan in their looks and ragged in attire, tended the engines, begged upon the road, or scowled half-naked from the doorless houses . . . .

Britain's unprecedented mass poverty was, without doubt, largely due to the high price of basic foods, especially bread. Yet it took two decades of Corn Law rule until an organized campaign against it began, and a group of northern manufacturers formed an Anti-Corn-Law-League. It made slow progress and there were a number of violent bread riots. At last, in 1846, the Government's hand was forced by the catastrophic potato famine in Ireland, and the Tory Prime Minister Sir Robert Peel realized the absurdity of forbidding the import of cheap corn while people were dying of hunger. Still the majority of his party refused to abolish the Corn Laws, but the Liberals came to Peel's aid, the Laws were repealed, and a period of free trade in foodstuffs began.

One of the most important steps towards modern agriculture was the development of artificial fertilizers as a result of the intensive research work carried out by the German chemist Justus von Liebig, the creator of organic chemistry. Taking his cue from Humphry Davy's suggestions in the first quarter of the century, Liebig investigated what the soil needed for producing the highest yield and for the restoration of its fertility. Natural farmyard manure, he found, was insufficient and varied too much to be of constant effectiveness; but artificial fertilizers could be chemically compounded from the required substances; mainly nitrate, ammonium salts, calcium cyanamide, phosphates, potassium salts in certain proportions.

Liebig's discoveries brought a new international industry for the production of chemical fertilizers into existence. As was to be expected, European farmers needed some time to overcome their

54

conservative mistrust of that newfangled kind of manure which was supposed to be better than the good old dung, and for which money had to be forked out; but the Americans took to fertilizers as quickly as they did to the first steam-driven harvesting machines. Both innovations made the cultivation of very large fields possible. Liebig, by the way, also invented meat extract, the most highly concentrated nutriment — and he was the first scientist to recommend special food for babies.

America's great new bounty of grain brought serious problems for European farming. As the nineteenth century neared its end, mechanized agriculture and steam navigation reduced the cost of imported grain from the United States, Canada, and Argentina so much that it could be sold in Europe considerably cheaper than the home produce. Canned fruit, vegetables and fruit from the other side of the Atlantic also competed successfully with the

Louis Pasteur (1822-1895)

indigenous, but uneconomically produced, fresh food. So long as European wages were low, the workers had to buy the cheapest stuff in the shops. Matters changed only gradually as European farmers adopted modern production methods from the turn of our century onwards.

Food preservation, however, was not a new technique; bottling had been invented around 1810 by a Parisian confectioner, Nicholas Appert, who won with it a prize offered by Napoleon for a method of prolonging the lifespan of certain foodstuffs for his soldiers and seamen on their far-flung campaigns. And it was another Frenchman, the chemist Louis Pasteur, who made canning safe at the end of the last century by his discovery of the micro-organic process that took place in organic matter, and by the development of food sterilization through heat treatment. The 'pasteurization' of milk, the preventive inoculation against chicken cholera, the discovery of the anthrax bacillus and the inoculation of humans to save their lives after being bitten by rabid animals — these were some of Pasteur's most important achievements.

How the Other Half Ate

Pasteur's achievement of sterilization was one of the two most important methods of extending the period of edibility of food; the other one, also introduced at the end of the last century, was refrigeration. Both systems are saving an enormous part of all foodstuffs from becoming unfit for human consumption.

Refrigeration owes its basic principle to Lord Kelvin's work on thermodynamics, especially on the mechanics of heat-exchange, which he developed. Mechanical refrigeration — the first ship equipped with it was a British one, the *Strathleven,* which began in 1879 to carry meat from Australia and New Zealand to England — depends on the 'refrigeration cycle'. A refrigerant is usually a liquid such as ammonia or freon, which turns into a gas at a comparatively low temperature; it absorbs heat from the food in an insulated chamber, and that low-grade heat is sufficient to vaporize the refrigerant. This is then pumped to a compressor where it gives up heat and condenses back into a cold liquid, which is made to pass through the food chamber again, cooling it. Thus the cycle is completed.

Much of the practical application of the Kelvin principle was carried out in the 1870s by Carl von Linde, a German engineer; but the general introduction of the refrigerator, in large storage rooms and in people's homes, had to wait for the development of the electric motor and for the building of large electrical supply networks around 1900. A later innovation was the absorption refrigerators, which can use gas from the mains or from cylinders instead of the electric current so that they may be installed in parts of the world which have no electricity supply.

By and large, the hungry years of the industrial proletariat were drawing to an end a century ago. But this did not mean that the working man and his family could begin to indulge in culinary luxuries: that was still the prerogative of the upper classes and the prospering bourgeoisie. In 1845, Disraeli had given his novel *Sybil* the sub-title 'The Two Nations' — the rich and the poor. Half a century later, towards the end of the Victorian era, there was no longer a 'great divide' between the lower middle and the working classes; for the life styles of the skilled engineer and that of the small shopkeeper or office worker were hardly different: a social development by that time caused by Britain's rise as a manufacturing nation. However, this had also created a new upper crust; that of the rich businessman, with a living standard as high as that of the land-owning aristocracy.

That upper 'other half' — in fact a minority, though typical of the later Victorian age — emulated the extravagant eating habits of the old aristocracy. Like all *nouveaux riches* they were snobs and admired the French cuisine with its reputation of being the most refined and accomplished in the world. Writers like Anthelme Brillat-Savarin — who published a gourmet's compendium and famous cooks like Marie-Antoine Carême — whom the Prince Regent engaged for his Brighton Pavilion — had done their best, in the early years of the nineteenth century, to persuade the civilized world that everybody who was anybody had to feed themselves the French way; pre-revolutionary of course. Queen Victoria and the Prince Consort too, had their French chef, and so had London's most exclusive clubs and restaurants. Ever since, high-class establishments have impressed their customers by writing their menus in French — though today their chefs may be Italians, Cypriots, or Austrians; or plain Englishmen. They all had to learn the French culinary jargon.

However, in spite of all their gastronomical pretensions, the upper-middle-class Victorians were gluttons rather than gourmets. We find some vivid descriptions of their meals in Dickens' novels; for instance in *Martin Chuzzlewit:* '. . . the table groaning beneath the weight of fowls, fish, boiled beef, roast veal, bacon, pies, and an abundance of heavy vegetables . . .'. The still famous English breakfast, with one or more hot dishes, tea, toast, and marmalade, took its characteristic form in those days; afternoon tea was often enriched by hot muffins, sold by street vendors who rang little bells, while the 'pieman' — his pies were filled with beef or mutton hash, eel or fruit — did his business usually in pubs.

A Victorian street vendor (Mary Evans Picture Library)

In Mrs. Isabella Mary Beeton's mid-Victorian classic *Book of Household Management*, published in 1861, we find many suggestions for bourgeois meals on various occasions. A 'simple' everyday family dinner would consist of four courses, e.g.: crimped skate and caper sauce, boiled knuckle of veal and rice, cold mutton, stewed rhubarb and baked pudding. For a dinner party with a dozen or so guests Mrs. Beeton suggests caviare, game soup, sea fish, curried prawns, wild duck ragout, roast turkey, fillet of beef with vegetables, snipe, golden jelly, and iced Nessel-

58

rode pudding. But even such a sumptuous meal, probably no exception in a prosperous businessman's household of the period (of course with innumerable servants), seems modest when compared to a private dinner given by Lord Palmerston for the Speaker of the House of Commons in 1865. Of this Disraeli recorded in his diary:—

> Dined with the Prime Minister who was upwards of eighty years of age. He ate for dinner two plates of turtle soup; he was then served very amply to a plate of cod and oyster soup; he then took a pâté; afterwards he was helped to two very greasy looking entrées: he then despatched a plate of roast mutton; there then appeared before him the largest, and to my mind the hardest, slice of ham that ever figured on the table of a nobleman, yet it disappeared, just in time to answer the inquiry of his butler, 'Snipe, my Lord, or pheasant?' He instantly replied 'Pheasant', thus completing his ninth dish of meat at that meal.

The miracle was that Lord Palmerston managed to live to such a great age on a diet like this.

However, not only the rich profited from the influence which the French cuisine gained over the western world's gastronomy. Britain's long coastline provided an abundance of fish — then at low prices — for the working population, brought inland by the railways from the middle of the nineteenth century onwards. Oysters, today regarded as a luxury, were so cheap that they ranked as a commonplace food for the poorer classes. By the early 1850s, London and other English towns had their first fried-fish shops, where cod or flat fish were sold with bread or baked potatoes. Twenty years later, these shops introduced a French invention — 'French fried', or chips. The success of fish and chips, a complete hot meal wrapped in newspaper to take away, was phenomenal among the working classes right from the start, and has remained Britain's most popular common man's dish ever since.

Food Rationing — a German Invention
Napoleon's idea of blockading a whole nation has been repeated in various forms in modern history, always with the idea of starving people into surrender. Britain as well as Germany blockaded each other from the beginning of the first World War in 1914, but the Germans, with their much shorter coastline, suffered more. Their ships, which should have brought a substantial part of their food and raw materials from abroad, were swept off the seas by the British Navy. Walther Rathenau, a leading industrialist, submitted to the Berlin government a plan for marshalling the

country's resources and supplies; he was appointed Economic Director of the *Reich* and introduced his own invention — food rationing on a national scale. Britain hesitated to follow suit. But at that time, 1916, Germany's U-boat campaign against British and Allied shipping began to have a serious effect on the United Kingdom's food supplies; millions of tons of which ended up at the bottom of the sea. So the Government created the first-ever Ministry of Food, but it was only in the last year of the war that rationing was introduced.

The situation was the same in all belligerent countries: farm workers had been drafted into the armies, the food supplies went with priority to the troops — in other words, former food producers had become privileged consumers, thus further restricting the food supplies for the civilian population. The shortages led to long queues outside the food shops all over Europe; yet the governments had to avoid any unrest among the people, for many of them were munition workers and civil defence officials who kept the home front in order. Rationing at least made sure that certain essential foodstuffs were distributed fairly and at controlled prices. England's civil population was certainly much better fed than that of her enemies, Germany and Austria; also, the British cooperated well with shopkeepers and authorities because they felt assured that everyone was treated alike. 'The food question ultimately decided the issue of this war,' declared Prime Minister Lloyd George.

Ration Queue — World War 1

But within a few years, Britain, the victorious country, was much worse off than it had been during the war — it was almost a return to the nineteenth century with its mass hunger and poverty. The only consolation was that the Continent was no less involved in the economic depression, which reached its greatest depths when America, too, was gripped by it in 1929, with dire consequences for the rest of the world. In Britain, food subsidies, tariffs for food imports, marketing schemes, Imperial Preference terms — all kinds of policies and regulations, often contradicting one another, were introduced, tried out, abandoned, forgotten. They did not help the unemployed; whose numbers rose to two and eventually three million. The General Strike of 1926, the Hunger March from Jarrow to London ten years later were sad 'signs of the times'.

Yet there were, in those inter-war years, some developments which raised hopes that things might, after all, change for the better. World food prices fell as a result of the crisis. Social welfare services were extended; in 1934, for instance, Britain introduced a 'Milk in Schools' scheme, which helped not only the children but also the farmers, increasing milk consumption from 40 to 100 million litres a year. Paradoxically, the last twelve months before the second World War were, at least in Britain, the most prosperous the workers had seen for two decades — for Hitler left no doubt in politicians' minds that he was bent on war. Rearmament was vital; never since the end of the first World War had industry been so busy.

When the new war began in 1939, two schemes were at once carried out by Britain — previous experience had shown that there was no point in awaiting the blockade of Nazi Germany and food rationing at home as a defence against the German counter-blockade. Again, a Ministry of Food was set up; already in 1938, the Board of Trade had been empowered to start with the storage of durable foodstuffs. Regional and local food authorities were established: decentralization was a sensible precaution as heavy air-raids and even invasion attempts were being expected.

Throughout the war, orange juice and codliver oil were available for children and pregnant women. School meals and factory canteen meals were provided in addition to the rations; restaurants, too, were ration-free, although there was a price ceiling per meal. On the whole, Britain's food rationing, 'points' and allocation systems were a great success, and there was not much of a black market; prices in the shops were kept low and stable by Government subsidies. The upper classes had to be content with less sumptuous meals than before the war, but the working population was certainly much better fed than during the lean years of the 1930s.

The lessons of the first World War had been learnt by both sides in the second. Despite Germany's large U-boat fleet, which inflicted heavy losses on the convoys carrying food to Britain, the blockade failed. But Germany herself was going all-out for breaking the Allied counter-blockade. In 1940, Hitler invaded three food-producing countries: France, Holland, and Denmark (plus Norway, but there fishing was rather restricted — the high seas were now a battlefield). In the following year, the great dream of the German 'geopoliticians' seemed to come true: the conquest of Europe's largest wheat-producing area, the Ukraine, for feeding Central Europe.

But the Soviets adopted a ruthless 'scorched-earth' strategy, and Germany got very little food from the Ukraine; the catastrophe of the German army at Stalingrad in the winter of 1942-43 — the turning point of the war — also marked the end of Hitler's *Drang nach Osten,* the 'drive to the East'. The last two war years were a period of increasing famine in Germany, of supply routes disrupted by Allied air-raids, and eventually of Allied advances from both sides. Even more than in the first World War, the lack of food played a decisive part in Germany's defeat.

Since then, the importance of food in politics has grown to vast proportions; we even have a new word for that new force — 'agripower'. It works both ways. Democratic governments cannot sanction or impose on their citizens, high food prices which would seriously reduce the people's standard of living. Authoritarian governments are in an even worse position when world market prices go up — dearer food at home may cause political upheavals endangering the stability of the countries' systems. Poland's rulers, for instance, had to capitulate over the issue of higher food prices in the early 1970s: the workers in the Baltic ship yards struck and rioted in protest, and there was some bloodshed. The Prime Minister and other top officials were replaced by new men who immediately withdrew the price-rise orders. This did not help the country's external financial problems, but at least there was peace at home — until another food crisis in 1976 triggered off riots again. At the same time, Egypt experienced a similar eruption of unrest, and there too a stabilization of food prices was forced on the government.

The other way in which agripower works in our time is less

obvious as it operates behind the international political and economic scenes. Many of the former colonial countries which achieved independence in the 1950s and 1960s had not yet reached a stage of development which enabled them to feed their citizens properly, and the wealthier nations pledged themselves to help them; especially through some of the agencies set up by the United Nations. Aid in the form of direct supplies, however, can be undertaken only by those nations which produce more than they need themselves — mainly the USA which, together with Canada, grows 80 per cent of the world's cereals. The temptation to gain influence on the developing countries and line them up as political allies by making them dependent on food supplies has proved irresistible to the power politicians.

We shall hear more about this, and about the agripower exercised by the new multi-national food corporations, in Chapter V. It may suffice to mention here two examples from the 1970s. One was the tragedy of Chile, where a new government which displeased the USA had come to power as a result of a left-wing election victory. At once, the food supplies from the USA were stopped — to be resumed only when a generals' junta had toppled the elected government, with bloodshed, mass arrests, and torture as the means of suppressing any opposition. The other conspicuous, but more beneficial example of international relations controlled by agripower, was the American-Soviet agreement on political détente based on grain supplies, which Russia needs desperately when her harvest happens to fail. But what is a 'friendship' of the two powerfully armed nations worth if it depends on climatic vagaries? The maintenance of détente, and with it of the peace of the world, may be influenced by the intensity of the snowfall in Siberia; if it is light, with good prospects for the coming farming year, the Soviets may think they can afford to cock a snook at their détente partners — with bad prospects for the amicable coexistence of East and West.

4

THE SCIENCE OF FOOD

'Unknown Factors'

When man emerged from the forests and caves and started out on the long road to civilization, he began to lose some of his animal instincts. One of them was the innate knowledge of what to eat and what to avoid. He had to learn it anew by experience; by trial and error. No wonder that his understanding of nature, and especially its edible parts, became overgrown by magic beliefs, superstitions, and old wives' tales, as we have seen. Only during the last century did scientists begin to take a closer look at the effects which our food has on us: of all the great branches of science, nutrition is one of the youngest.

Before the body's 'fuel', our food, could be investigated, the exploration of the human anatomy had to provide the basic knowledge of how our organism works. The Church had strictly prohibited the cutting-up of corpses, and it was long after the Reformation that doctors dared to do it for the study of anatomy. William Harvey, court physician to James I and Charles I, discovered how the blood circulates in the body. At the end of the seventeenth century, Robert Boyle — the pioneer of modern chemistry and especially biochemistry — overthrew the ancient doctrine of the four 'elements' and 'humours' ruling human bodies, with its unlikely application of food and health. Boyle showed that acids, salts, alkalis and so on were of real importance in our organism. A hundred years later, the great French chemist Antoine Lavoisier studied the way in which the body turns food into energy and muscular power.

For the first time, the measurement of the energy value of food was then expressed in 'calories', units of heat. Two other terms, now familiar to us, emerged during the last century: proteins and carbohydrates. It was Justus von Liebig, the German biochemist, who analyzed these vital components of food. Proteins are organic compounds containing carbon, oxygen, hydrogen, and nitrogen; they are essential parts of all organic matter, and we get them by consuming meat, eggs, milk, cheese and certain vegetables. Carbohydrates are also compounds of carbon, oxygen, and hydrogen; but in different proportions. They are contained in starch and sugar. Fat is also necessary for man's diet; we get it from butter and vegetable oil as well as from fatty meat.

Nineteenth-century scientists knew that people's well-being depended on a number of additional inorganic and mineral substances — iron, phosphorus, calcium, iodine, potassium and others — all contained in various foodstuffs. Yet the knowledge of nutrition still had great gaps. For centuries, scurvy — with its weakening demoralizing, and sometimes lethal effects on sailors during long voyages — had been fatalistically accepted. Captain Cook recognized it as the result of a dietary deficiency and at the end of the eighteenth century the British Admiralty ordered the supply of citrus fruit juice for all its ships. The great success of this innovation, which put an end to scurvy in the British Navy, pointed to the existence of some hitherto unknown biological factors.

Still, another century passed before European scientists began an investigation of those 'unknown factors'. They found that there were several kinds, all of them important for people's health, but each consisting of a different substance. A major discovery in this research work was that the debilitating disease beriberi (from the Singhalese word for 'infirm') was widespread in those areas of the Far East where 'polished' rice — with its husks removed by milling — was a staple food. As early as in 1881, the Japanese conquered beriberi among their ships' crews by supplying them only with unpolished rice. In Britain, the biochemist Sir Frederick Gowland Hopkins found, early in our century, that milk contained the same food factors as rice husks, and that they were also present in whole-grain cereals, yeast, and offal. By that time, those factors had already been given a name: vitamins.

Their discovery did not create a popular sensation, as one might have expected; people had been brought up on the idea that diseases could be caused by something one ate, not by the absence of certain invisible elements in their food. To be sure, codliver oil had been forced down children's throats for quite some time because it had been found that it guarded them against rickets and strengthened their bones; but the general idea of a well-balanced diet, which includes vitamin-rich food, did not take root in western countries until the 1920s, and then first among

65

the middle and upper classes. A leading British nutritionist, surveying the food scene in the 1930s, came to the conclusion that over half the population lived on a vitamin-deficient diet by force of habit, not because of poverty.

As we have heard, the second World War — with its food shortages all over Europe — stimulated some governments to take action, especially to provide children with vitamins in the form of milk, orange juice, and other vitamin-rich foodstuffs. Today, these notions are commonplace, and the practical application of nutritional science entails the provision of vitamins as a matter of course. Each vitamin, or group of vitamins, has been assigned a letter of the alphabet; their chemical structures have been analyzed, and most of them can now be produced synthetically to be added to certain manufactured foods or prescribed for patients suffering from vitamin deficiency. Here is a table of the most important vitamins showing their natural sources and the ailments likely to develop if there is a lack of them:—

Vitamin	Natural Sources	Deficiency Symptoms
A & A1	Fish-liver oil, liver, milk, cheese, eggs, butter, green vegetables, carrots	Diminished growth, skin eruptions, night-blindness, changes in the eye
B1	Unmilled cereals (rice, wheat), barley, oatmeal, eggs, liver, milk, legumes	Growth impediment, polyneuritis, beriberi, gastro-intestinal ailments
B2 (a complex of several vitamins)	Meat, fish, liver, yeast, leguminous seeds (beans, peas, lentils), whole wheatmeal, egg-white, milk. Intestinal microbes also produce B2 vitamins	Symptoms vary according to the kind of B2 vitamin lacking; e.g. pellagra, hair loss, dermatitis, changes in the cornea
C (ascorbic acid)	Fresh lemons, oranges, limes, grapefruit, rose hips, green salad	Scurvy
D (sterol compounds)	Fish-liver oil, fresh vegetables, butter, milk. Sunlight produces vitamin D in the body by ultra-violet irradiation of the skin	Rickets, softening of the bones
E	Wheat germ, leafy vegetables	Muscular distrophy, sterility, changes in the kidney
K	Cabbage, spinach, cauliflower, fish-meal	Lowering of the coagulation power of the blood, changes in functioning of the liver

Another scientific discovery of the nineteenth century, whose immense practical importance was not recognized until the beginning of the twentieth, was 'Mendelism'. This biological theory of heredity in plants and animals was propounded by an Austrian monk, Johann Gregor Mendel. He came from a family of peasants, but was able to study at the University of Vienna and after graduating he entered the Augustine monastery at Brno in Moravia, where he became a science teacher at the monastery school and eventually Abbot. Mendel's passionate interest was biology; which was making great strides in the wake of Darwin's work. In his little allotment in the priory garden he planted edible and sweet peas, trying to discover the natural laws of inheritance; with the aim of breeding plants with certain characteristics by selective fertilization. The laws he established — regarded as no more than a scientific curiosity during Mendel's lifetime — made the breeding of plants and animals with superior qualities possible: grain

Gregor Mendel (1822-1884)

immune to rust, cows with greater milk yields, chickens laying more and larger eggs, to mention only a few of the benefits of Abbot Mendel's work.

Twenty years after his death in 1884, 'Mendelism' — which can be defined as an applicable system of heredity, with the recurrence of inherited characteristics reduced to numerical laws — was generally accepted and practised in agriculture. But then the term was gradually fading out of common usage, to be replaced by a new one, genetics. Today we have come a long way from the monk's one-man garden laboratory. Genetics means the study of heredity and variation by delving into the micro-world of chromosomes and genes, it also means the modern technique of breeding. But some danger lies in 'genetic engineering', as the deliberate manipulation of selective genetic breeding is called. To be sure, it brings us the most useful animals; but most people probably feel that we should stop geneticists from trying — as they no doubt will — to produce super-humans with masterminds, fit to rule the world, by genetic engineering. Mankind may prefer to do without them, and to carry on muddling through by trial and error, as it has done for the last half-million years.

The Great Leap in Agriculture
American farming has contributed the major part of the general increase of the world's food production in recent times. During the last half-century, U.S. wheat yield has gone up from 1.1 tons per hectare to 2.1 tons, and maize yield from 2.4 tons per hectare to 5.7 tons. Since 1950, America's overall agricultural productivity has risen by almost 50 per cent. The country's vast areas of good soil and a climate favourable for grain growing, an efficient engineering industry which furnishes ingenious farming machines, a sophisticated .chemical industry which produces excellent fertilizers and pesticides — these are the main factors which have made America the world's biggest food supplier.

Perhaps the most important element in that farming revolution has been the attitude of the farmers themselves. While the rural population in Europe and much of the rest of the world, proverbially allergic to any change in its work and lifestyle, clings to its traditional methods, the American farmer believes in progress, in scientific advances, in modern technology. A hundred years ago, U.S. farming was mainly manual work with the hoe and scythe, supplemented by the muscle power of oxen, horses, and mules. The great leap in productivity began with the mechanization of agriculture. Steam engines had been tried out in the fields early in the nineteenth century, but they proved to be unsuitable because of their weight, cost, and cumbersome operation. But after the invention of the mobile, petrol-powered internal-combustion engine (by the German engineers Benz and Daimler) in the mid-1880s and of the heavy-oil-powered engine (by another German engineer, Diesel) ten years later, the road to farm mechanization was open. The Americans, with their enormous 'corn belt' from Ohio to Nebraska, developed tractors for ploughing, harrowing, seeding, and harvesting, and for hauling mowers and binders, as well as stationary engines for driving fodder and dairy machines.

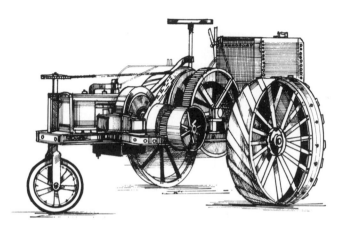

Early tractor, manufactured in 1902

The American food crisis of 1916 gave a great impetus to tractor design — with Henry Ford as the chief pioneer — while the British Government sponsored the development of its own tractor models to increase food production during and after the first World War. Soviet Russia, in the grip of widespread famine in the post-revolutionary years, made the design and mass production of tractors its overriding priority. Then came the introduction of the combine harvester in America; the machine which cuts and threshes the grain and puts it into sacks or tanks as it travels through the fields. Whole armadas of these machines are a common sight in the corn belt at harvest time. Eventually, mechanization began to extend to livestock husbandry, with milking-machines and chicken-rearing and egg production in 'battery'-type barracks where the birds spend their lives in small compartments, being fed from a moving belt. However, many people decry the quality of chickens and eggs produced in this way; efficient as it might be, and pity the poor hens which are never allowed to feed and roam in the open air.

Some big farms in the American mid-West operate automated systems which go even further in the interest of labour-saving. Fleets of tractors, with implements attached, are remotely controlled by button-pushing and switch-pulling and move without human drivers. These plough and sow, fertilize and harvest the crop, and finally empty it into glass-lined storage silos. Other buttons are pressed at cattle-feeding time and a scientifically measured amount of fodder goes down an elevator shaft into troughs, already mixed with supplementary vitamins, antibiotics, and hormones which help to fatten the animals faster and protect them from diseases. Like the battery hen, they are never allowed outside their air-conditioned byres and styes — except the cows which have their daily exercise hours. Automatic machines also kill, pluck, clean, and package the chickens.

This kind of dehumanized — and, as some crities call it, callous — farming is, of course, practicable and profitable only in a country with wide open spaces as the investment in automatic installations is enormous. But other products of modern food technology reach our tables day by day, and often we are hardly aware of what we are actually eating. The oldest item of 'manufactured' food, the sausage, has always been a popular butt of ridicule because the consumer could never be sure what that cylindrical envelope actually contains. Already 2500 years ago, Aristophanes made a joke about it in his comedy *The Clouds.*

Sausages are supposed to consist of some kind of chopped meat, spiced and often eked out with breadcrumbs or other cereal matter (e.g., oatmeal), and enclosed in a short length of animal gut. The *botulus* of the ancient Romans (which gave its name to the dangerous botulism — food poisoning from sausages or tinned meat) was always sure of a laugh in a farce; English medieval mummery and eighteenth-century harlequinades featured strings of sausages as objects of fun. No other culinary speciality appears in so many varieties and under so many names — from the Frankfurter and the British 'banger' to America's hot dog and Scotland's haggis, from Italy's salami and mortadella to Munich's 'white' sausage and Vienna's vienna, and from Spain's *chorizo* to France's *boudin*, an equivalent of England's black pudding. Today, sausages are rarely still made by individual butchers, at least not in the industrialized countries, where they are mass-produced in huge quantities for customers who have little time for cooking a meal and not much money to spend on food.

'Food industry' — today a household word in the literal sense — is a term that would have sounded absurd only a hundred years ago. Strangely enough, it was Napoleon III, otherwise not renowned as a ruler with a social conscience, who suggested scientific research into the possiblity of manufacturing some kind of cheap substitute for butter for the working classes. A French chemist came up with a formula for such an artificial fat, with beef tallow, milk, and minced cow's udder as the main ingredients. Dutch dairy farmers took up the idea, improving the mixture by adding vegetable oils, and the Americans began to mass-produce it in the late 1870s. Soon it was also exported to Europe under the trade name of 'butterine', later to be renamed — for some still unexplained reason — 'margarine', from the Greek *margaron,* pearl. pearl.

Because of its initially unappetizing taste amd smell, it was not an immediate success, but manufacturers who recognized the great marketing possibilities of the new substitute spent much money and effort on its improvement. Later, some government authorities ruled that the natural vitamins of butter — A and D — must be added to margarine as it had become a regular part of the family diet in countries with a large industrial proletariat. Today, oils from a wide variety of plants (palm, maize, groundnut, coconut, sunflower, soya) are being used as ingredients, plus whale oil and milk powder. The substitute has improved so much that perhaps consumers cannot distinguish it from butter, as the advertising slogan claims. Although the price difference between the two is small, it may play some part in a big family's budget. Among the middle classes, margarine is often used because of the cholesterol 'scare' — doctors say that animal fats may cause an excess of this organic compound in our blood, which can clog the coronary arteries, but vegetable and fish oils do not.

Since the introduction of margarine, many more manufactured foodstuffs — called 'convenience foods' — have found their way to our tables, most likely for social as well as for economic reasons. The changed role of the women in our western society, within and outside the family, has caused a marked tendency to reduce to a minimum the time spent in the kitchen. Until the first World War, the domain of most middle-class women was the house in general and the kitchen in particular; then came their gradual emergence as joint breadwinners with the men, due to economic necessity, and their emancipation as individuals with jobs, careers, professions in their own right. Working women want and need as much leisure time as working men; so the hours formerly spent on cooking had to be reduced, if possible, to minutes.

The manufacturers responded to that tendency, providing foods that did not require preparation from scratch. The oldest kind of cooked food preserved in metal cans was meant mainly for soldiers, sailors, and explorers. In the 1860s, however, a Mr. H.J. Heinz in Pittsburgh was probably thinking of ordinary cooks and housewives when he marketed cans of dried, grated horse-radish; the first of his proverbial '57 varieties'. Today, processed food in tins and jars is complemented by frozen meat, fish, vege-tables; by packaged soups, sweets, and cake mixes, and by com-plete pre-cooked dishes in cartons and plastic bags, available in the industrialized countries at supermarkets and village grocers alike, and ready for the table within minutes. Altogether, these convenience foods are estimated to amount to about one quarter of the entire expenditure on food.

Modern convenience foods

Another time-saving innovation are the take-away shops and restaurants; the modern successors of the old public cookshops where the poorer classes could get cheap, ready-cooked meat. In Britain, the fish-and-chip shops had been a long-established source of prepared hot meals, but the bourgeoisie regarded them as too proletarian for their taste. The Chinese caterers in Britain, most of

72

them from Hong Kong, started a new trend by transplanting the Eastern system of take-away meals to the West in the 1960s and the Indian restaurants were quick to follow; now, Italian pizzas and Turkish kebabs can also be taken away in heat-preserving tinfoil containers, to be eaten at home. No doubt, the attractions of these ready-cooked meals for the housewife are not only the time and labour she saves but also the exotic variety of the food, and last but not least the advantage of instant dinners for the family while they are watching television.

It may be argued that all these modern aids for the housewife are killing the art of cooking. But that art cannot flourish anyway when the women are severely limited in the time and labour they can spend on regularly feeding their families. A true artist will always find a chance to exercise her creative urge — say at the weekend when the work-day pressures have eased — and cooking 'something special' for the family or guests may be an even more tempting task if cooking is not an inescapable daily drudgery. The enormous sale of cookbooks with recipes from all over the world is a most encouraging sign. Also, one cannot expect all women to be devoted cooks; but some men are, and the weekends give them a chance to prove their talents too.

Food Technology: Boon or Bane?

Early in the last century, a London printer sold many copies of a home-made poem listing the worst deceivers in the food trade:—

> The first is the miller with his dusty head;
> he sells you the flour to be made into bread,
> mixes whitening, bone dust, and other bad things,
> and I'm sure of all rogues he must be the king.
> The baker comes next who is honest no doubt,
> until that his tricks are fairly found out;
> he'll swear that his bread is made of the best flour,
> only mention 'tatoes and alum you'll make him look sour. . .

And so the poem goes on, accusing the grocer of selling horsebeans for coffee and sloe leaves for tea, and the dairyman of milking not only his cows but also his water pump. These were by no means exaggerated accusations by a man who had been cheated and wanted to let off steam — that amateur poet had the backing of several scientists who were investigating food frauds. The most notable of them was a German-born chemist living in England, Frederick Accum, who published his *Treatise on the Adulteration of Food, and Culinary Poisons* in 1820.

Accum had taken the trouble of analyzing a wide range of foodstuffs which were being sold to the general public; particularly to the workers. Hardly an item in his report was given a clean bill of purity. Alum was indeed used to whiten flour and not only dried leaves of sloe but also of elder and ash, curled and coloured on copper plates, were used as make-weights in tea. Pickles were coloured green with poisonous dye while copper and lead salts were used to embellish sweets with rainbow hues for children; the 'nutty' flavour of wines was achieved by means of bitter almonds (which contain prussic acid); cheap tea was made to look 'Chinese' by treating it with poisonous verdigris; pepper was 'watered down' by adding pea flour, mustard husks, and juniper berries; and the rind of Gloucester cheese was made to look more attractive by colouring it with red lead.

The manufacturers and traders attacked Accum viciously, and he was practically driven back to the Continent. Still, the public had been alerted, and some of the food fakers mended their ways. But twenty years after publication of the *Treatise* a new scandal broke: eight London factories were found to be specializing in making old tea new — they collected dried, used tea leaves from hotels and restaurants, added colouring matter, and resold them to dealers. Another twenty years went by before Parliament passed the first, relatively mild Food and Drugs Act.

Nowadays, food adulteration is liable to severe punishment in all civilized countries; yet from time to time there are still sensational scandals. In 1969, for instance, an Italian cheese producer was found to have sold grated Parmesan which, in fact, consisted mostly of the grated handles of derelict umbrellas. Also in Italy around the same time, wine of the chianti type was analyzed as a concoction made not from grapes but largely from banana skins; while in neighbouring France a whole vintage of Bordeaux wines was found to be heavily adulterated with chemical liquids.

Modern food technology has developed efficient methods for preserving prepared and packaged foodstuffs; but these methods entail the use of additives which, to the food purist, appear as abominations. In most western countries they have to be listed on every package, though manufacturers prefer to do so in rather small print. Reading through a magnifying glass, the consumer who buys a packet of instant soup may find that it contains, besides nourishing ingredients, chemicals such as monosodium glutamate, calcium silicate, hydrolized protein and yeast hydrolysate. Monosodium glutamate was the object of international warnings in the late 1960s; it is a 'taste powder' made from seaweed, which has been used for ages in the Far East to savour

74

dull food. But some people are allergic to it, and the American manufacturers of baby food decided to stop using it as it might harm the health of small children.

A modern health food shop

The food purists condemn all additives, especially in bread, which some of them like to bake themselves. They are horrified that things like chalk, for instance, are added to bread flour. In fact, this is done to improve its nutritional value; other additives prolong its lifespan — while the purists' home-baked bread may go stale much sooner. Harmless ingredients of some foodstuffs enhance their smell, appearance, or taste. Jam is stiffened, drinks are made more homogeneous by additives; anti-caking agents prevent salt, milk powder and instant coffee from becoming lumpy, 'sequestrants' stop fats and oils from going rancid. An expert committee set up by the United Nations produced a report on additives in 1966, setting certain standards for food manufacturers and assessing the good or harm which additives may do.

Yet some of the purest natural foods may also have harmful effects. Sugar, for instance, ruins the teeth and can be the cause of heart trouble through overweight if it is not consumed sparingly, and it is poison for diabetics. An alternative sweetener is saccharin, a chemical compound discovered a century ago; weight for weight it has 550 times the sweetening power of sugar but no calories at all. A related sweetening agent is sodium cyclamate, widely used in manufactured soft drinks. France has always banned the use of cyclamates, and in 1970, the U.S.A. and Canada did the same after scientists had found that large doses of the stuff produced cancer of the bladder in rats. Another substitute for sugar, widely used in soft drinks, is isoglucose, made from maize. It is considered harmless, but the European beet-sugar growers want it banned.

There is no synthetic substitute for salt — not yet, anyway. Since the beginnings of cooking, salt has been valued as an essential natural additive and a powerful preserving agent. Yet many people believe that it is harmful; after all, common salt (NaCl) is a compound of the metal sodium and the green, poisonous and ill-smelling gas chlorine. A salt scare started in the 1920s when German doctors warned certain groups of patients, especially sufferers from tuberculosis, against salting their food. For healthy people, however, salt is as harmless as it is essential for their bodies' water economy. A saltless diet may cause them to lose their appetite, among other deficiency symptoms.

Over-anxious eaters may shrink from innumerable foodstuffs when they hear what potential poisons they contain: spinach and rhubarb have oxalic acid which could produce kidney stones; liquorice might lead to high blood pressure, carotene (present in carrots, egg yolks, mangoes, sweet potatoes) to jaundice, onions to anaemia. Tea and coffee, lima beans and bitter almonds, nutmeg and avocado pears — they all contain toxic substances, and even cabbage may do you harm: it could produce goitre. Once you start looking for poison in your food, there is no end. Things are, however, much worse for those who decide to opt out altogether of our synthetic life style and live 'close to the earth', feeding only on the plants it offers. A young man who had been leading such an existence in the English woods in 1977 ended up in hospital after a few days, seriously ill. When he had recovered

76

he showed the doctor the plant he had eaten; it was hemlock. 'People who want to live off the land,' said the doctor, 'may easily die off it.'

Some who believe in the mystique of 'closeness to nature' are worried that the poisons from chemical fertilizers may find their way into foodstuffs. For these people, health shops cater with food grown, under guarantee, only with the help of natural manure. But what is natural manure? In the farmyard, the dung heap is the traditional source of the elements necessary for plant growth, organic (and some inorganic) matter important for soil fertility. They are contained in animal excreta, poultry droppings, vegetable compost, and waste to a widely varying extent: they are chiefly nitrogen, phosphorus, potassium, sulphur, calcium, magnesium and a host of other elements in minute amounts. The list shows that it is the chemical constituents which the plant requires for its growth, whether they come from a chemical works or the rear end of an animal.

A characteristic example is guano, which is found in great masses on the Pacific sea-shores of South America. It is the excrement of seagulls, cormorants and penguins, with nitrogenous and phosphatic compounds, plus some potassium and ammonium salts, as its main constituents. It is an excellent natural fertilizer, up to 30 times more effective than ordinary farmyard manure. As early as in 1840, guano from islands off Peru was shipped to Europe. But when Peru banned the export of guano a hundred years later, this mattered little to countries with chemical industries — they could easily produce guano-like synthetic fertilizers. In the developing countries, of course, imported natural manure (such as guano from the Gilbert and Ellice Islands) may play an essential part in agriculture.

In the western world, the hankering after foodstuffs grown with the help of natural manure is therefore slightly eccentric. The censorious comparison of modern farming methods with the good old days is no more than a romantic whimsy; in fact, adulteration and food fraud have ceased to be as rife as in the past since governments introduced stricter laws, with public analysts watching over food production.

Genetic Pest Control
Is there more justification in the fear that residues of chemical pesticides may get into the food they are supposed to protect?

Plant pests and diseases still affect much of the world's food supply; fungi alone destroy every year enough crops to feed

300 million people, rats and spoilage in storage ruin even more. So long as man subsisted on wild-growing plants, they were in a natural balance with plant-eating insects; but the cultivation of plants with higher yields also favoured the spread of pests. Some of the most destructive are cunning travellers, such as the Colorado beetle. After eating whole crops of potatoes in the South-west of the USA it invaded Europe, crossing the Atlantic in potato transport ships. Only the strictest watchfulness and chemical insecticides can beat such a foe, which may destroy the potato crop of hundreds of square kilometres of farmland in one season.

Pest control: spraying of crops in India. Inset left: Colorado beetle. Inset right: Locust.

Environmentalists, however, believe they have a strong case against chemical pesticides; they quote the notorious story of DDT. This chlorinated hydrocarbon pest-killer — which was discovered in 1874, but whose insecticidal powers were not recognized until 1939 — has become a classic example of boon turned into bane. DDT was used extensively and highly successfully in fighting the dangerous epidemics that were spreading in Italy at the time of the Allied landings in 1943; three years later, large areas of Ceylon (Sri Lanka) were sprayed with DDT to eradicate the malaria-carrying mosquitoes. The disease was as good as stamped out and the island's death rate was drastically reduced. Similar experiences with DDT were made in British Guiana.

But then came the backlash. Residues of DDT were found in the human body, in cow's milk, and even in the flesh of Adelie penguins and of crab-eater seals captured in the Antarctic. Still worse, other species of pests had developed since DDT and other insecticides had destroyed their natural enemies, and some harmful insects had become immune to the control poison. Rare birds and animals were in danger of extinction as a result of the disturbance of the ecological balance by chemical agents; for example, after DDT had been used to kill off the black gnats of Clear Lake in California, the plankton of the lake was found to have been destroyed as well, fish which used to feed on the plankton died, and so did the grebe — diving birds which had been feeding on the fish.

Since then the geneticists have worked out their own methods of pest control. Their idea is that of making insects die out by rendering large numbers of males sterile. They are mass-bred, sterilized by X-rays or gamma rays, and then released. Females mating with them have no offspring, and thus the insect population is quickly decimated.

The first large-scale field test of another system, which uses the frequent 'incompatibility' of male and female insects from different regions, was carried out in a village in Burma, under the auspices of the World Health Organization (WHO), in 1967. 'Incompatible' male mosquitoes from another region were bred in laboratories; 270,000 of them — heavily outnumbering the local males — were released over a 12-week period around the village. The incompatible couples did not produce any offspring, and eventually the village was completely mosquito-free.

Genetic control systems seem to offer several advantages over other methods, especially over chemical ones. Costs are low; application does not pollute the environment and leaves no residues. Genetic systems are 'specific', meaning that they affect only the target species and no other organisms. Last but not least, pests may develop resistance to chemical attacks, yet they are unable to resist genetic methods of extermination.

Efforts to control farm pests by biological methods are still in a trial-and-error stage, and unexpected effects may occur, as in one of the first attempts at controlling a plague of rats in the sugar cane plantations of Jamaica. Mongoose were brought to the island; they did contain the rats in a short time, but multiplied so much themselves that they became a danger to domestic animals. The case showed that it may be easy to manipulate the ecological balance by biological methods, but difficult to restore it if the experiment fails.

Today, scientists accept the fact that ecological principles have to be applied right from the start of plant cultivation. The method which is now favoured is called 'integrated plant protection', a synthesis of biological and chemical pest control coupled with agricultural systems such as crop rotation, synthetic fertilizers and soil conditioning. Special attention is being devoted to the water economy which must not be upset by such measures as large-scale deforestation. Unspoilt nature has its own 'water-builder' which offers an excellent solution to a number of problems — the beaver. His wooden structures dam up the fast-flowing rainwater, thereby raising the level of the ground water which favours the growth of vegetation along the rivers. For this reason, beavers are now being released again in many North American districts where they had previously been hunted and decimated; it is hoped that the beavers will rehabilitate river areas which were destroyed by man in his greed and folly.

But to return to the human species: what determines a people's choice of food? First, of course, there are the geographical factors — the climate, the kind of soil in which certain foodstuffs grow best, the seasons when they become available to the population. Religion and cultural traditions come next. The whole social structure of a people is another factor which not only influences its food habits but is also influenced by them. The development of transport and other technical facilities — for instance, fishing boats or salt-trade routes — affects the choice of food to a great extent. And there may also be some as yet little explored hereditary factors. whole tribes or even nations show likes and dislikes which may have their origins in nutritional needs or allergies. For example, the absence of milk in the diet of many Asiatic nations — particularly the Chinese — is due to their lack of the digestive enzyme called lactase, an organic catalyst which breaks down lactose, the milk sugar. Drinking milk would make them sick, though they are not allergic to dairy products such as butter, cheese, or yoghurt, which contain practically no lactose.

Revolution in the Kitchen
Throughout the Middle Ages, most of the common people of Europe lived in houses that consisted of little more than a single

room, often with a mud floor; in winter, a wood fire was lit in the middle of the room for warmth and for cooking. In summer, the cooking was done outside, at least when it was not raining. In England the Norman barons introduced a slightly more civilized way of life in their castles; the 'keep', the domestic part of the building, had a walled fireplace where the cooking was done. The smoke escaped through the windows — unglazed holes in the walls. Later, the mansions of the noblemen and the monasteries were built with large kitchens; the royal palaces had hearths big enough to roast two or three oxen on spits, often turned by dogs in treadmills. The Italians, being a music-loving nation, invented turnspits which played tunes.

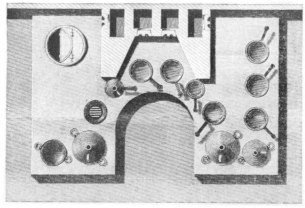

Elevation and plan of Rumford's kitchen range (1789)

A great change in kitchen design came when coal began to replace wood as the common fuel in the seventeenth century. Coal provided more concentrated heat, and so hearths could be made smaller; metal was now used for all kitchen utensils which were exposed to the heat. The age of the open hearth, without proper outlet for the smoke and waste heat, was coming to an end, and that of the kitchen 'range' began.

The man who designed the prototype of the enclosed range which was to be used throughout the nineteenth century — and which is still the basic form of our modern electric and gas stoves — was Count Rumford, the American-born statesman, scientist and reformer, the founder of domestic science (see Chapter II). He had the first scientifically constructed kitchen range installed in the Munich house of a nobleman in 1789. Robert Southey, the English writer and historian, saw and described it:—

> The top of the fire is covered with an iron plate, so that the flame and smoke, instead of ascending, pass through bars on the one side, and there heat an iron front, against which food may be roasted as well as by the fire itself; it passes on heating stoves and boilers as it goes, and the smoke is not suffered to pass up the chimney till it can no longer be of any use. On the other side is an oven heated by the same fire, and vessels for boiling may be placed on the plate over the fire. The smoke finally sets a kind of wheel in motion in the chimney, which turns the spit. I could not but admire the comfort and cleanliness of everything about the kitchen.

The ordinary domestic version of Rumford's range was, of course, much less elaborate.

A Scottish engineer, William Murdock, who worked in James Watt's steam-engine factory, invented gas light at the beginning of the nineteenth century; but it took another forty years until gas was used for cooking for the first time. That was at a Leamington Spa hotel when a hundred guests were treated to a dinner cooked on a large gas oven. Strangely enough, the idea did not catch on till after the introduction of electric lighting thanks to Edison's development work. Then the gas industry, worried about the new rival power, made great efforts to market gas cookers, and by the turn of the century these were well on the way to superseding the coal-fired kitchen range. One of the decisive steps in popularizing the gas cooker among English middle-class householders was the introduction of the slot meter which made payment for the used gas easy and painless.

But the electrical industry was also determined to keep its foot in the kitchen door. The first electric cookers for ordinary kitchens

82

were exhibited in London in 1891, and two years later a complete electric kitchen was one of the sensations of the Chicago World Fair — with electric range, broiler, and kettles. The general public, however, regarded these innovations as too advanced for everyday use, and there was a widespread fear of high-voltage currents. Even electric lighting, first installed by Edison in a New York street block in 1882, was met with a good deal of suspicion.

Electric cooking grew popular only in the 1930s; after the second World War a number of new electric appliances for the kitchen offered help to the housewife: rapid-action kettles and hotplates, infra-red grills and spits. Modern contact grills which, using very little fat, transfer the heat to the meat at temperatures not much higher than the boiling point of water, effect an even penetration of the food without shrinkage or weight loss; automatic control enables the housewife to let the meal cook itself; time switches and temperature controls (thermostats) make sure it does not burn to cinders. Microwave ovens are also popular, because they use little electric power and reduce cooking time.

What, in fact, are we doing when we cook food by radiating, convecting, or conducting heat? Science has made us understand what, in the past, was a matter of trial, error, and experience: the physical and chemical changes which make raw food easy to chew and to digest as well as more palatable. Most important of all, heat destroys harmful bacteria, particularly in meat. Cooking softens the connective tissues around the muscle fibres; starch grains swell and burst their walls so that our digestive juices can act on them more readily; the cellulose fibres and cell walls of vegetables become tender. Cooking makes more foodstuffs edible and even the smell of cooking and of cooked food is beneficial — it stimulates the glands which produce saliva, the fluid which aids mastication.

Of course, we eat much of our food uncooked and cold, such as fresh fruit and salads; but there are in the western world raw-food addicts who eat nothing but foodstuffs in their natural state — though few of them would go to the extreme of picking their own plants like the poor fellow who ended up in hospital with hemlock poisoning. The raw-eaters exist on a rather limited diet as many food items become digestible only after cooking. They are the radical sector of the much larger group of general vegetarians, whose ideas go back to antiquity — Plato and Plutarch were advocates of vegetarianism — or are based on ethical, medical or religious concepts. In the eighteenth century, Rousseau believed in meatless living on moral grounds, and so did Shelley in the early nineteenth; in the middle of that century, the movement grew in popularity, and today it is quite widespread. But the vegetarian's belief that his way of life makes him a better man does not necessarily hold good — after all, Hitler was also a vegetarian.

As a rule, vegetarians abstain from any food obtained by the killing of animals, though some draw the line at fish, which they eat, while others include even eggs among the foods of animal origin from which they abstain. Most vegetarians avoid the use of animal fats and of meat extracts. They believe that vegetables, cooked or as salads, supply them with enough vitamins and mineral salts, and wholemeal cereals, beans and flour with sufficient protein. The health reasons which many vegetarians give for their dietary choice are that flesh-eating is responsible for serious diseases like cancer and tuberculosis and for heart trouble caused by overweight.

Anti-vegetarians argue that man is by nature omnivorous, that his stomach and intestines have been developed to draw nourishment from anything that is edible, and that otherwise he could not have survived as a species. The vegetarian, they say, must eat a large quantity of food to obtain sufficient nutritional values, as too much of what he eats is excreted as waste products. Another argument is that vegetable meals are less appetizing than ordinary ones, and as a result the vegetarian may be chronically undernourished.

But this is perhaps preferable to becoming too fat — the most common harmful condition in the richer countries today. It shortens life by causing heart troubles and other serious ailments. Gerontologists point out that the greatest percentage of centenarians live in the Soviet Republic of Georgia, most of them vegetarians whose traditional diet consists mainly of fresh vegetables, vitamin-rich herbs, honey, milk, and cheese; another country where people are said to live to a great old age is Bulgaria, the land which gave yoghurt to the world.

The problem of obesity was first brought to popular attention in 1863 by an English cabinet-maker, William Banting, with his *Letter on Corpulence*. At the age of 66, he wrote, he had reached a weight of 100 kilograms; then he devised for himself a strict diet of non-fattening meals without milk and sugar: tea, dry toast, and up to 140 grams of meat (except pork) for breakfast; up to 170 grams of fish (except salmon) and vegetables (except potatoes), some poultry, and 2-3 glasses of dry wine for dinner and supper. Within a year or so, he lost over 20 kilograms in weight. Many people emulated him and adopted his diet, which was called the 'Banting system'.

Most modern slimming diets are based on Banting's principle of giving the body enough nutriment while keeping the calorific value to a minimum. A typical example, recommended by doctors today, is the 'high-vitality health diet': fruit juice with honey, some wheat germ cereal, a raw egg, and yoghurt for breakfast; raw salad with sunflower seeds or cottage cheese, followed by yoghurt with honey for lunch; fruit or vegetable juice, lean meat, grilled fish or nut rissoles, with some cooked vegetables and green salad for dinner. Those who feel peckish between meals may drink some clear vegetable broth. This diet supplies 1000 to 1300 calories a day, compared to the 2500 to 3000 calories of the ordinary plentiful meals we eat if we don't have to worry about our weight, especially if we use up a lot of calories in physical work.

Prevention, of course, is even better than cure, which means in nutritional terms: a regular 'balanced' diet keeps people reasonably healthy and in good trim. The notion of balance in eating is comparatively new; it gained popular interest and appreciation only after the discovery and evaluation of the vitamins — when people who had never given much thought to their food suddenly realized that their meals might be lacking certain vital ingredients while they were stuffing themselves with calorie-rich food. That new understanding caused a minor revolution in the kitchens of the western world.

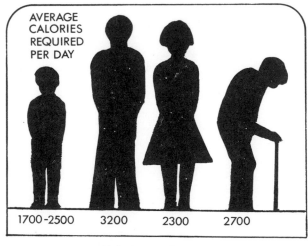

Calorie requirements

85

Normally, hunger acts as a guide to the amount of calories needed, which varies with an individual's age, height, and daily physical activity. Children need more calories to maintain their growth than an adult who works at a desk throughout the week, and manual labourers need more than old people whose metabolism — the biochemical processes by which foodstuffs are turned into energy — has slowed down. Calories are supplied to the body by carbohydrates (contained, as we know, in starch and sugar), fats, and proteins (contained in meat, milk, fish, eggs, cheese, cereals, nuts, peas, beans, and lentils). Carbohydrates are needed by the body for providing energy (also in the form of heat) and materials for building blood cells, enzymes, hormones and other substances, also for repairing worn-out tissues. Equally important are of course vitamins and mineral salts; and drink is needed to give the body — which consists of 75 per cent water — enough moisture.

The pattern of a balanced diet varies with people's ages, occupations, national traditions, the climate, the availability of foodstuffs, and often religious rules. However, here is a rough chart of a well-balanced diet in a temperate zone and for families in average financial circumstances:—

FOOD	WHAT IT SUPPLIES
Cooked meat, fish, liver	Protein, fat, vitamin A & B, iron, calcium, phosphorus
Bread (if available, wholemeal)	Carbohydrates, protein, vitamin B, iron, calcium
Milk	Milk sugar, vitamin A, B & D, protein, fat, calcium, phosphorus
Eggs	Protein, fat, vitamin A & B, iron
Vegetables (incl. potatoes), salads	Carbohydrates, mineral salts, vitamin A & C, roughage (bran)
Soups, gravy, beverages, soft drinks	Water, vitamins, carbohydrates or fats
Fruit, fruit juice	Grape sugar, vitamins, mineral salts
Cheese, nuts	Protein, fats, vitamins
Butter, margarine, corn oil	Fat, vitamins A & D

5

THE FIGHT AGAINST FAMINE

A New Look at the Food Scene
A decade or so after the end of the second World War, when its worst ravages in Europe had been mended, the western nations and the new international agencies of the United Nations turned their attention to the permanently hungry areas of the globe; mainly in South-east Asia, Africa, and South America. In 1961, the Food and Agriculture Organization (FAO) of the UN launched a 'World Campaign Against Hunger' with the double aim to ensure that people throughout the world would be made aware of the problem of hunger with its attending afflictions, human misery and human degradation; and to 'create a climate of opinion which will contribute to the solution of these problems on a national and international level'. These aims were to be fought for within the general strategy of the FAO, which had taken on the responsibilities of 'raising the levels of nutrition and standards of living of the underprivileged peoples of the world' and of 'securing improvements in the efficiency of the production and distribution of all food products'.

How much nearer to achieving their aims have the UN progressed during those last decades? To be sure, a great deal has been done. The 'have' nations pledged themselves to give aid in money and in kind regularly to the 'have-nots'. African and Indian villagers have been trained in modern farming methods, South American peasants have been taught animal husbandry. Irrigation of deserts has stopped soil erosion, land has been reclaimed for cultivation, forests have been planted, fishing co-operatives started, agricultural machines supplied, new crops introduced, and new generations of veterinarians have been trained.

But soon after the great Campaign against Hunger had got into its stride, a new danger was identified and given a new name: population explosion. That spectre prompted the question of whether even the most efficient and comprehensive modern methods of food production would be sufficient to keep pace with the rapid increase of hungry mouths which needed to be fed. At the 1963 World Food Congress in Washington, the British historian Arnold J. Toynbee said:—

> War, pestilence and famine have been the three traditional scourges of the human race. They have been Nature's brutal ways of keeping the human population of our planet within limits. . . . If we are to defeat these three scourges not just momentarily but definitely, once and for all, we have to win a fourth victory. We have to conquer some of our most intimate and most deeply ingrained habits, traditions and prejudices. We have voluntarily to regulate our birth rate to match the regulation of our death rate that we have already been achieving.

When Professor Toynbee said this, the world's population was estimated at three thousand million; within the next fifteen years, it rose to over four thousand million. We should be horrified; yet we have no reason to panic. For during that same period, developments have changed the world food scene completely.

Already in 1945, the Finnish chemist Artturi Virtanen, who had just won the Nobel Prize, expounded his theory that by the year 2000 the population of the world would reach six thousand million, and that thereafter the rate of increase would decline — while food production could be stepped up to feed eight thousand million people. In Europe, he pointed out, agricultural yield had risen from 700 to 3,500 kilogram per hectare since the end of the Middle Ages; in the USA, it had roughly doubled during the first half of the twentieth century (see Chapter IV). By the end of this century, biochemistry and technology would be easily capable of doubling the whole world's food production again.

Thirty years after Virtanen's predictions, his claims were endorsed by numerous expert and authorative statements — at the third World Food Congress in Rome in 1974, by the International Wheat Council, by the Select Committee on Overseas Aid of the British House of Commons in 1976, and in a number of well-researched books and media reports in the mid-1970s. All these sources indicated that the general public's way of thinking about the world food situation would have to be thoroughly revised to keep up with the facts and figures that had emerged.

There are now only two basic facts which have remained more or less unchanged: the hunger of hundreds of millions of undernourished people and the shocking over-consumption in the rich countries, which Lord Boyd Orr, the first Director-General of the FAO, had once called 'the doubtful pleasure of eating ourselves to death'. An overall estimate of 500 million undernourished people in the world does not seem too high; but the total of the population in the developing countries amounts to well over 2,500 million people, about two thirds of the total world population. This shows, according to the German Professor Uwe Kracht, Nutrition Officer of the FAO, that in wide areas of the developing countries there has been a good deal of improvement, and that new cultivation methods of cereal crops have resulted in unexpectedly high production increases. Within five years, for instance, India's wheat production rose by almost two thirds, and Pakistan's by over 80 per cent. Yet this is only part of the whole picture.

The greatest surprise of the mid-1970s was a simple comparison between two statistical figures; in the three decades since the end of the second World War, the global population had increased by 70 per cent; but the world's food production had risen by well over 150 per cent! For the first time in history, it had reached an annual figure of 1250 million tonnes. India's and Pakistan's wheat 'miracle' was reflected in the figures from other developing as well as developed countries; altogether, the world's annual wheat harvest was exceeding 400 million tonnes.

What, then, had gone wrong? Why were those 500 million people — mainly in southern Asia and Africa — still suffering from an overall calorie deficit and, to a large extent, also from an insufficient supply of protein? Why were the developed countries, whose inhabitants account for only one third of that of the whole world, consuming over half of its food, and why were they being constantly 'troubled' by food surplusses for which they could not find consumers? Another absurdity was that the animals in these countries were allowed to eat the equivalent of one quarter of the total grain consumption of the people of India and China put together. Or, in the impassioned words of the Egyptian President of the World Food Council, the new decision-making body of the United Nations, set up in 1975: 'Are we to say that the world, which can send a man to the moon, which can cure the majority of diseases and can produce machines to solve the most complex mathematical problems within seconds, can still deny millions of its inhabitants sufficient food to keep them alive?'

One sad fact was emerging more and more clearly: the aid programme, the charitable help which the developed (and the rich oil-producing) countries were giving to the hungry ones, had failed. It was obviously impossible to provide the essential daily minimum of 2200 calories per head merely by occasional shipments of crumbs from the rich man's table. Even if the developed countries decided to cut their own consumption drastically, say by 20 per cent, and let the famine-stricken parts of the world have it, those 500 million underfed people would get, at best, 2-3 per cent more to eat; the children would still be suffering from kwashiorkor, due to lack of protein, vitamin, and albumen, and their young adults from marasmus; premature physical senility.

One reason for the inadequacy of the aid given to the developing countries is that much of it gets lost. Corrupt administrations in those areas are known to have sold food consignments to businessmen; potentates and ministers have simply pocketed aid money to pay for their own luxurious living; and some governments have used it for prestige projects such as magnificent official buildings in their countries' capitals — as claimed in the 1976 report of the British Parliamentary Committee on Foreign Aid, which called for measures to ensure that international financial aid is principally used for rural improvements. In 1977, Britain's Minister for Overseas Development told an audience of Congressmen in Washington that aid money must be prevented from being used 'cynically by ruthlessly repressive regimes as a means of bolstering their authority'.

Other reasons for the waste of food aid were listed in the FAO report of 1976. Food worth almost five million dollars had been lost through pilfering, bad storage, and careless distribution, with the result that many people died who should have been kept alive. In other cases, gifts of food were sent to the wrong people, such as the four million oranges shipped to a remote Indian famine area; they were left to rot because the inhabitants had never seen that fruit before and were afraid to eat it. An American foreign-aid plan which has come in for much criticism is the 'Food for Peace' scheme. It sounds admirable: providing low-interest, long-term loans to poor countries so that they can buy surplus food from America. But, as the *Washington Post* wrote in 1977, the scheme 'has been accused of helping to keep certain governments in power, of creating food gluts to the detriment of local farmers, and of making countries dependent on the United States for food while failing to develop their own crops'.

'Agribusiness' — A New World Power

The failures of many aid schemes for the needy nations, however, do not entirely explain why in our age of greatly increased food production there is still so much starvation in the world. Some experts say that much of the blame must be laid at the doors of the new giant corporations, the 'multinationals', which have become rulers in the realm of 'agribusiness' — combining food production and trade, processing and distribution; they are increasingly taking over from individual farmers and cooperatives, from wholesalers and shipping companies.

The label 'multinational' is usually applied to a company which operates in half a dozen or more countries and sells goods for over 1,000 million dollars a year; there are now an estimated 200 of these giant corporations, which have developed since the 1960s. They deal in all kinds of fields, from motor-cars and transistors to armaments and food, producing altogether about one sixth of the world's goods and services. Why have they spread over so many countries in several continents? Because it is cheaper to produce goods in under-developed regions where wages are low, while the customers for these goods are mostly found in the more prosperous industrialized countries where people have money to spend. The profits are therefore enormous.

What interests us here is the part played by the multinationals in food production, trade and distribution. To begin with, these corporations acquire the control over large production areas. According to United Nations statistics, only 2.5 per cent of the world's landowners now control almost three quarters of the total arable land — and most of these 2.5 per cent are not individual farmers but giant corporations. Many are based in America, but some have their headquarters in Europe; for instance a British one which began its phenomenal rise as a simple sugar-refining firm, and a Continental one originally dealing mainly in condensed milk and chocolate. Today, they rule over vast realms of food production, transport, and distribution.

We can easily see why the multinationals prosper at the cost of the poorer countries. At the World Food Congress of 1974, some speakers put it in the simple words: 'They grow cheap and sell dear.' By their sheer size and wealth they can put the basic forces of the capitalist market system, supply and demand, out of action; it is the corporations which can dictate the prices, make certain goods scarce, manipulate the food trade.

The critics of this agribusiness say that one of its most harmful features is the tendency to re-shape the 'geography' of food production the wrong way to make it more profitable. To quote a notorious example from the early 1970s: at the height of the famine in Ethiopia, which claimed 100,000 victims, a study group went to that stricken country to investigate the prospects of starting low-quality meat production — for the pet-food industry in the western hemisphere. In the Philippines, a multinational corporation grows exotic fruits of which only 10 per cent are eaten locally while the rest is exported to the USA and Europe as luxury foods. In Mexico and the poorer South American areas, asparagus and strawberries are being grown for the same customer countries, and South-east Asia provides the tables of the Japanese rich with delicacies.

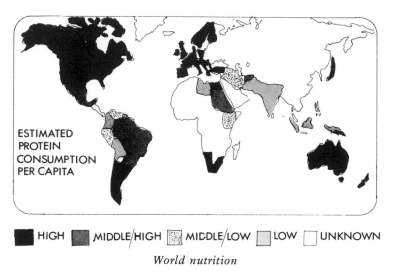

HIGH MIDDLE/HIGH MIDDLE/LOW LOW UNKNOWN

World nutrition

The poverty of the tea workers in Sri Lanka (Ceylon), who supply much of the favourite drink of fifty million Britons, seems to contradict the laws of economic life. In 1977, Dr. K.A. Hassall, of the University of Reading, put the blame fairly and squarely on agribusiness when he wrote:—

The shameful fact for us is that the vast bulk of such crops is grown for profit and not to benefit the hungry, and that the profit goes in part to the shareholders in multinational firms and in part to a landowning or administrative elite (often with political influence) in the developing countries themselves. . . . Who owns or leases the large estates is unimportant to the increasing number of displaced subsistence farmers who cannot then even grow their traditional protein-rich pulses. . . . The irony is that while a developing country may grow tea, coffee, sugar, or high-yield wheat for a lucrative export market at prices above the reach of the local

92

population, the dietary standards of those who grow that food may actually decline. . . .

Unless a method can be found to share more equitably the benefits of the Green Revolution, capitalism could only too literally sow the seeds of its own destruction by creating conditions leading to political instability in much of the Third World.

As we see, the problems we know from history — such as the upheaval caused by Britain's Agricultural Revolution two centuries ago — are still with us, only on a world-wide scale in our time. Then as now, it is up to a new generation which has not yet lost its compassion and conscience to find solutions and to right the wrongs inflicted on our fellow human beings by a short-sighted, profit-minded age.

The Common Market

Although world production of food now increases, as we know, faster than world population, birth control is still essential. Campaigns to encourage it in the developing countries have had only limited success; population growth in Latin America, Africa, the Middle and the Far East (except China, which pursues its own strategy but publishes no statistics) is at present 2.4 per cent a year, as compared to about 1 per cent in Europe and North America.

It is common knowledge that the lower a nation's standard of living, the higher is its birth rate. This vicious circle must somehow be broken, and the first aim should of course be to bring the poorer countries up to a level of self-sufficiency in basic foodstuffs. But this is a field where many cardinal mistakes are still being made. In 1976, the U.S. Foreign Agricultural Service published a survey showing that out of 50 food-importing countries, 46 were applying policies which 'directly or indirectly, discourage food production for their own populations'. We have quoted some examples of schemes started by the multinationals which are guilty of similar results, but even international organizations that are independent of the profit motive make them as well. Take, for instance, a project backed by the World Bank in Kenya.

There, 'subsistence herders' like the Masai, Samburu, and Turkana are encouraged to become commerical ranchers, producing meat for the European market. Obviously, if this is a viable way of producing meat, it should be first and foremost used towards the goal of making protein-starved Kenya self-sufficient. On the other hand, there is a massive scheme to make the most populous part of a whole continent, with about 250 million inhabitants, as self-sufficient as possible. It is called the European Economic Community (EEC), the Common Market for short. Is it a success?

Its history goes back to 1923 when a Dutch-Greek-German politician, Count Coudenhove-Kalergi, started a 'Pan-European' movement with the aim of establishing a United States of Europe. Thus, he argued, wars in the old, strife-torn Continent would become a thing of the past, political and economic cooperation would supersede the traditional rivalries, and a unified Europe would become in world politics a factor as powerful as the United States of America. However, Europe was clearly not yet ready for unification, Hitler and the second World War then put an end to the scheme for the time being.

It was revived in the 1950s in a new, more practical form by the governments of six western and Central European countries:

Map of the Common Market

94

Western Germany, France, Italy, the Netherlands, Belgium, and Luxembourg. The Treaty of Rome, which they signed in 1957, envisaged the gradual elimination of all import duties and trade restrictions amongst the Six and a common tariff for imports from the outside world. The economic cooperation of the member states was hoped to increase their bargaining power in dealing with other countries, and a common agricultural policy was expected to create a fair balance between the foodstuffs produced, consumed, exported and imported by the EEC countries. Long-term aims were a European Government, a common currency, and common laws — in other words, the complete merger into a single European nation.

These were the lofty yet practical targets of the Common Market, which was in 1975 enlarged by the accession of Great Britain, the Irish Republic, and Denmark to membership. Still, the Count's Pan-European ideal was not fulfilled; the main difference is that eastern Europe, with its vast grain-producing areas, has been left out. Now, one of the cornerstones of the EEC is its Common Agricultural Policy (CAP), the administration of which is based in Brussels; its basic problem is to find common denominators for the member countries' individual interests.

This has turned out to be rather difficult, for each country has its special agricultural structure, developed over the last two centuries or more. Britain, for instance, has a highly developed, very efficient system of farming, yet has to rely for half of her food on imports from overseas (formerly supplied mainly by her colonies); France's farmers have always refused any thorough modernization of their production methods; Italy has never been able to strike a balance between the fruit-growing south and the industrial north, which needs considerable food imports; Holland and Denmark, on the other hand, are economically dependent on their exports of dairy produce; Germany's agriculture is still characterized by small-scale farming, especially in the south. None of these countries has been willing, or able, to adjust itself to the demands of a Common Agricultural Policy as worked out by the administrators in Brussels, where the 'farm lobbies' of production areas with widely conflicting interests are trying to pull the CAP officials this way or that.

The results, as every housewife in the EEC countries has found out, are not very encouraging. A complicated system of price controls, import duties, and subsidies has been developed, but the expected benefits for producers and consumers have not materialized. On the one hand, the cost of living throughout the EEC rises continually; on the other, mountains of unsaleable butter, milk powder, and meat are accumulating, oceans of milk and wine are waiting in vain for buyers. From time to time, butter is being sold at a fraction of its price within the Common Market, to the Soviet Union and other countries. Italian and French vintners are at each others' throats; some of their wine has been poured into the rivers, some has been turned, at great expense, into industrial alcohol. Fruit and vegetables have often been dumped on dung-hills. The CAP system does not permit low-price sales of all these marvellous gifts of nature to the population of the Common Market countries.

So the great European experiment in central food-policy planning seems to have failed. Yet sooner or later, some sensible international control system of food production and distribution will have to come if mankind wants to avoid the dangers of world-wide food shortages; the scandal of food going to waste in one part of our planet while people die of hunger in other areas cannot go on indefinitely. Social and political unrest is bound to arise. What the world needs is a really powerful control organization, with 'teeth' for enforcement, to ensure the equitable distribution of food products at unmanipulated prices which the needy can afford. This would, of course, entail the restriction of the power and influence of governments as well as of the multinational corporations. It would also mean the enforcement of a fundamental change in land ownership, in the control of the international food trade, and — last but not least — the establishment of food reserves for emergencies. A beginning has been made with FAO's project of a 'grain bank'. An even more imaginative suggestion was made, back in 1956, by Admiral Richard Byrd, the leader of the U.S. Antarctic Expedition: to use the Antarctic continent as the world's surplus food store — a natural deep-freeze installation which needs no energy and little maintenance, ready for any emergency; it could hold 500,000 tonnes of food stock.

Food for the Future
Despite the encouraging recent developments, we cannot rely on a continuing growth of food production at a greater speed than the increase of the world's population. Nor is there any certainty that the disappointingly slow training of new farming generations in the developing countries will quicken. And there is the greatest problem of all, the imbalance in the distribution of food; it cannot be solved without a powerful international control body which could enforce its decisions upon big business and governments alike.

But what about the large autocratic states outside the Euro-American orbit, the Soviet Union and China? They will, no doubt, have increasing influence on world food affairs in coming decades. In the Soviet Union, the production of grain has also expanded faster than the population as in many other parts of the world. Yet despite this encouraging general trend, Russia's food fortunes have always vacillated between bumper crops and harvest failures due to climatic adversities such as droughts, and the Soviet government needs some insurance against the danger of famines — not only among its own population but also in its allied East European countries which it has to supply with food for political and strategic reasons. Therefore, it concluded the agreement with the USA, which we have already mentioned, to buy an annual minimum of six million tons of grain, come rain, come shine: the agreement that also guarantees a political détente between the two world powers and rivals, so long as it holds. The Soviets have also embarked on a massive irrigation programme; their ultimate aim is, according to official statements, to provide each citizen in every 'normal' year with at least 60 kilograms of meat; a large horse-meat sausage plant is also being built.

China's people seem to be well-fed at present, but the leadership wants to avoid any emergencies which would force them to buy basic foodstuffs from abroad. One of the country's most famous schemes is the 'Tachai Brigade', established in the 1950s. Tachai is an agricultural training centre some 300 kilometres south-west of Peking which is visited by an average of 2500 people a day, mindful of their late Chairman Mao's admonition, 'Learn from Tachai'.

There is a resident team of no more than 450 people — the élite of China's agricultural research workers and pioneers. They have remodelled the land around Tachai, terracing and draining it against floods, and cultivated wheat, maize, and sorghum with the most advanced means. The result is that Tachai yields are now eight times higher than in the first year of the centre. The level of mechanization is high, but it has been achieved without government investment — 24 per cent of Tachai's income from sales of its produce is re-invested in machines, seeds, fertilizers. The aim is to convert China's 750 million peasants, most of them still working their private plots, to the high-quality collective farming developed at Tachai.

Another often-quoted watchword of Chairman Mao's was: 'One man, one pig', and China is well on the way towards that ideal. The pig, first domesticated in that country about 7000 years ago, plays an enormous part in agricultural life, not only as a supplier of protein and fat, but as a 'small organic fertilizer factory', according to Mao: 'If we could achieve one pig for every inhabitant, the fertilizer problem would be solved.'

Today, China has nearly 300 million pigs, that is one third the number of inhabitants and 40 per cent of the whole world's pig population; the Soviet Union has only 72 million and the USA 55 million of these useful animals. Pork is the most popular meat in the Chinese cuisine and, according to Communist Party philosophy, a 'key factor in the class struggle' because pig-raising is more practical on collective farms than for individual citizens, and collectivization is regarded as the ultimate aim in agriculture.

In striking contrast, a marked new trend among the U.S. population is a movement of 'liberation' from the greengrocer by growing one's own vegetables and fruit in the back garden. It all began during the energy crisis of 1974, when petrol prices soared and inflation got a strong new impulse. Today, according to the U.S. Department of Agriculture, well over half of all American households, nearly 40 million, have some kind of kitchen garden, or at least a few window boxes for growing fruit and/or vegetables. There are many seed firms, including some large mail-order companies which provide the amateur farmers with fool-proof instructions as well. Several hundreds of thousands of prefabricated green-houses have also been put up in citizens' back gardens, often replacing that old status symbol, the swimming-pool. Gardening has become fashionable, last but not least because the exercise it involves is considered an antidote to the stresses and strains of modern life — and to overweight.

An American development of considerable importance for the outside world is the phenomenal rise of soya bean production and export. It is a very ancient leguminous food plant, cultivated by the Chinese nearly 5000 years ago, according to the earliest records. But it was only in 1908 that soya beans were first brought to the west, to England. During the following two decades some American farmers planted it, though merely for hay and for ploughing under as manure. Then the nutritionists began to experiment with it, growing new varieties and developing new harvesting and processing methods. The seeds of the bean were found to contain 18 per cent of high-protein oil; the first large-scale utilization of soya was in the form of meal as livestock feed.

After the second World War, the demand for soya from the cattle-raising countries rose to such an extent that many U.S. farmers took up soya-growing as a speciality. At present, half of

98

Soya bean

America's soya crop is being exported as oil or meal; in industry it is being used for paints, soap, pharmaceutical drugs, cosmetics as well as in leather and textile manufacture. It is now an ingredient of margarine and confectionery, ice-cream and bread (and we know it well as the flavouring sauce for Chinese meals). But its main use may come in the near future; British education authorities have introduced it as a cheap but valuable source of protein in school meals, and the high price of meat is bound to encourage its widespread use in the everyday diet of the western countries.

The necessity of providing enough protein for mankind is one of the central food problems. The surveys of the FAO show that about one third of the world's population is suffering from protein deficiency, and the search for exploitable new protein sources is a vital task. Obviously, the increased use of the oceans is very much in the nutritionists' minds. 'Single-cell proteins' (SCP) are another new research field: the term covers proteins based on yeasts, bacteria, micro-algae, micro-fungi, and protozoa — in short, animal as well as vegetable sources.

Israel, with its chronic shortage of foreign currency, has embarked on a large SCP development programme to reduce its annual import of 330,000 tons of protein for animal fodder, but also with a view to creating new foodstuffs for its human population. A pilot plant for producing SCP from methanol has already been set up; it turns each ton of methanol into ½ ton SCP, 75 per cent pure, for replacing imported livestock and poultry feeds.

Africa's problems are bigger and more pressing. The protein shortage affects many millions of the continent's population. Perhaps the most comprehensive research work in this field has been carried out by a Nigerian biochemist, Professor O.L. Oke of the University of Ife. Nigeria is a good example of the African situation as it is not only the largest of the newly independent countries (with a population of about 80 million) but also contains a wide variety of communities with different social backgrounds, tribal and religious traditions, and stages of development.

But what most of them have in common are, apart from protein and vitamin deficiencies, superstitious beliefs which impede nutritional progress. Eggs, for instance, are supposed to cause diarrhoea in children and 'make them become thieves later in life'. Artificial feeds for babies, too, are said to cause diarrhoea — 'which, of course, is due to the unsanitary methods the mothers employ', says Prof. Oke. Meat and fruits are supposed to give children worms, and they are not allowed to eat these foods. In the northern region, pregnant women are eating only cattle meat in the belief that this will cause the pregnancy period to be exactly nine months, whereas goat meat will reduce it to 7 and camel meat extend it to 12 months. Education will have to eradicate these superstitions.

The lack of sufficient protein is the cause of kwashiorkor, which is responsible for a high infantile mortality rate. Only about half the children born alive reach the age of 5 years; among the under four-year-olds, infant mortality in the different regions varies from 19 to 35 per cent.

The most popular staple food in Nigeria is cassava, eaten in the form of *gari* (fermented cassava). 'If we really want to cater for the poor people,' says Prof. Oke, 'so that they can eat enough good food, then it is time we stopped treating symptoms and go straight on to attack the diseases — that means changing to vegetable proteins. Cassava is an excellent source of energy but is virtually devoid of protein. But there are alternative starchy roots with better nutrients, e.g. yam, sweet potato and cocoyam. Nature has also endowed us with the possibility of producing high-protein concentrate from micro-organisms and from green leaves, systems that are 10-100 times faster than breeding livestock.' Fish, 90 per cent of which is preserved by smoking, could supply great quantities of sorely needed protein to the inland regions, but transportation and distribution facilities are still quite inadequate. The obvious answer to the problem, says the Professor, would be the installation of freshwater fish ponds in as many inland towns and villages as possible.

Leaves are a great untapped source of protein. Nigeria's sugar-cane, sweet-potato and pulse plants are ideally suited as their leaves, normally burnt or ploughed in, contain between 20 and 40 per cent protein. However, much development and especially promotion work among the population, which is still largely unaware of its dietary deficiencies, has to be done, says Oke, before Nigerians — and millions of other Africans — are adequately nourished.

At an FAO conference in the 1970s the protein production from yeast and bacteria was discussed from the technical angle. These sources can best be utilized by cultivation on hydrocarbons, where those micro-organisms multiply fast, and petroleum is the most important hydrocarbon medium. If only 5 per cent of the world's annually extracted crude oil was used for protein production, said an expert, this would provide the protein-starved peoples with 44 million tons of it. But he was well aware of the difficulty of diverting any oil from its present industrial uses. 'This would require a concerted action,' he said, 'as massive as the Manhattan Project which produced the atom bomb!'

A considerable potential exists in the cultivation of micro-algae as protein sources. Certain kinds of these proteins have already found applications in the food and other consumer industries, but their potential for future nutrition is enormous. With their protein content of 70 per cent, the spirulina algae could yield up to 32 tons of protein per hectare — 100 times the yield of wheat and 60 times that of soya beans. Food researchers are already thinking in terms of synthetizing complete foods based on the protein from micro-algae, which also contain several essential vitamins.

An unconventional source of protein for small children has been discovered among the rural population of northern Thailand. An enquiry into the feeding of village children between 3 and 5 years old, showed that at least 85 per cent of their intake of calories is met by foods with a high carbohydrate content such as sticky rice, which is eaten with some wild-growing vegetables — plus a small amount of protein-supplying little creatures: tiny fish, mussels, and frogs. But this is not sufficient for the health of the children, who suffer from deficiency ailments like kwashiorkor.

The problem is similar in the South American mountain regions where livestock breeding is difficult because of lack of protein-rich fodder plants. Here, the remedy might be the cultivation of lupins — not for the cattle, but for human consumption. But these plants would have to be selected from the low-alcaloid varieties which are not too bitter. Lupins have a high protein and oil content, and they like the South American highland climate. The inhabitants, who are undernourished, may be easily persuaded to grow lupins and include them in their protein-poor diet, say the nutritionists who have studied the situation.

There is no doubt that new nutritional sources have to be found for the undernourished areas of the globe and as emergency foods for preventing the worst effects of crop failures. One project which is commanding world-wide interest is the exploitation of the krill, a tiny shrimp-like creature, 4-6 cm long, and plentiful in some Antarctic waters; nutritionists have called it the earth's largest and so far hardly recognized provider of protein. The krill, very rich in albumen (soluble protein), has served the sperm whales as their staple food — but now that man's greed and folly have seriously depleted the whale population through over-fishing, the krill are multiplying as never before. Japan and the Soviet Union have been using the krill tentatively in various forms: raw as an *hors d'oeuvre,* processed into a sandwich spread, cooked or baked into fish fillets or as an ingredient for soups and sauces. Early attempts at introducing krill dishes in Europe did not meet with much success among customers, but German cooks discovered that what makes krill unpalatable is the contact with hot fat. They worked out a variety of dishes accordingly, and a department-store restaurant in Bremerhaven treated its customers to them for a whole week in 1976, without getting any complaints about the taste.

The necessity of providing enough protein for mankind lies at the heart of the whole food problem. The search for new protein sources is therefore vital. Also important is the cultivation of new land. The Dutch have increased their arable soil by reclaiming one quarter of their present mainland area from the sea in a vast operation begun in 1923. But for many other countries, especially in tropical or sub-tropical zones, irrigation is the key to survival.

British engineers have developed some new methods of what is now called 'water resource technology'. A team worked out a great water-sharing scheme in the Indus Basin, divided through the centre by the border between India and Pakistan; five rivers were involved. Today, the tributaries of the Indus provide all-year irrigation and electric power to 70 million people. Computers were used to build up a rainfall pattern for Ghana, where the new

Irrigation project — Tunisia. On the left side of the open drainage ditch is an irrigation channel

Barikese Dam fulfils similar functions. On the Ivory Coast, an Anglo-French team of engineers designed the Bandama Dam for nearly 80 million cubic metres of storage water; the scheme irrigates a vast new sugar-cane estate. British engineers also developed water supplies for the Mecca region, with a sewerage disposal system to eliminate the danger of epidemics caused by pollution.

Israel, with its steadily growing population and its severe economic problems, has to exploit all its natural resources to the full with the help of advanced scientific and technical methods, and with the aim of achieving self-sufficiency in food. Its large southern part, the Negev, is still mainly a desert. The government has embarked on an ambitious scheme to make it bloom by the 1990s, populated by 100 to 150 new settlements. High hopes are placed in a recently developed desalination system, producing fresh water for irrigation from sea water at a cost which is said to be 30 per cent less than the cheapest existing process. Coordinated with this is a system of drip-irrigation of grain fields, which saves water by avoiding loss through evaporation and permits fertilizers, mixed with the water, to be fed directly to the plant roots. Water-responding new grain varieties have been developed, producing very high yields under controlled irrigation.

Other advances in this sphere are sprinkler irrigation for orchards, switched on and off automatically according to the humidity of the soil; radio-controlled irrigation systems for large kibbutzim through underground pipes; and the re-use of waste water from citrus and vegetable processing plants for irrigation. Much research is also devoted to the techniques of 'hydroponics'; growing crops without soil, only in water impregnated with chemicals.

But there is a chance that mankind will derive much of its food from another new source, if science realizes one of its most cherished dreams: the artificial emulation of the way in which plants produce carbohydrates such as sugar and starch from the air's carbon dioxide and water in the presence of sunlight. It is called photosynthesis. If this can one day be done in the laboratory and then in factories, our food habits may change very much indeed.

So will they if, as some nutritionists predict, our western society will all but stop eating meat and fish. Two thirds of our cereal harvest, they point out, is now being fed to animals, which consume 2½ times more food than they produce; farming has 'degenerated into an animal-feeding industry' — a luxury which we may not be able to afford much longer. Even fishing in the open sea needs 10 calories of energy for every calorie of food it provides. Meat and fish may price themselves out of the ordinary consumer's reach, and we may all turn into vegetarians perforce — getting out protein from cereals, vegetables, oil, seaweeds and the like, skilfully mixed, processed, spiced and disguised as steaks and fillets.

However, we can merely survey the alternatives to our present-day food habits, but we are unable to predict which of them will become the dominant factor of tomorrow's food scene. Science and technology may come up with achievements which we cannot yet foresee. But one thing may be certain: that the dismal prophecies of some science-fiction writers will not come true in this or the next century — about mankind living mainly on pills and tablets with concentrated nutritional chemicals. If it ever comes to that it could only be in the very distant future, for it would mean that man himself has to change physiologically so much that he no longer requires any bulk food for his alimentary organs. As

104

we said at the beginning of this book, creatures have themselves to change in order to survive a fundamental change of their milieu, and this is a long evolutionary process in which only the fittest species make the race while the others die out. Pill-eating man may not be man at all but some new breed of ethereal creature.

So let us enjoy food, let us enjoy cooking and eating and drinking as long as we can, and let us see to it that our fellow-men can enjoy it too.

ACKNOWLEDGEMENT

Author and publisher wish to thank the librarians of the Department of the Environment, London, and Prof. O.L. Oke, of the University of Ife, Nigeria, for their special help with the compilation of material for this book.

BIBLIOGRAPHY

Aykroyd, W.R., *Food for Man* (Pergamon, 1964)

Barrons, K.C., *The Food in Your Future* (Van Nostrand Reinhold, 1975)

Bender, A.E., *The Facts of Food* (OUP, 1975)

Borgstrom, G., *World Food Resources* (Intertext, 1973)

Boyd Orr, Lord (ed.), *Feast and Famine* (Rathbone, 1957)

Burnett, J., *Plenty and Want: Diet in England* (Nelson, 1966)

Chambers, J.D. and Mingay, G.E., *The Agricultural Revolution 1750-1880* (Batsford, 1966)

Clair, C., *Kitchen and Table: A Bedside History of Eating* (Abelard-Schuman, 1964)

Ferguson, S., *Food* (Batsford, 1971)

George, S., *How the Other Half Dies* (Penguin Books, 1976)

Hammond, J.L. and B., *The Village Labourer 1760-1832* (Kelley, 1913)

Kleyngeld, H.P., *Adoption of New Food Products* (Tilburg University Press, 1974)

Larsen, E., *An American in Europe: Count Rumford* (Ryder, 1953)

Marei, S.A., *The World Food Crisis* (Longmans, 1976)

Pyke, M., *Food and Society* (John Murray, 1968)

Pyke, M., *Technological Eating* (John Murray, 1972)

Salaman, R.N., *The History and Social Influence of the Potato* (CUP, 1970)

Tannahill, R., *Food In History* (Eyre Methuen, 1973)

Wilson, C.A., *Food and Drink in Britain* (Constable, 1973)

INDEX